Frank Bromilow

Butterflies of the Riviera

A short account of the Rhopalocera of the Maritime Alps

Frank Bromilow

Butterflies of the Riviera
A short account of the Rhopalocera of the Maritime Alps

ISBN/EAN: 9783743407114

Manufactured in Europe, USA, Canada, Australia, Japa

Cover: Foto ©Andreas Hilbeck / pixelio.de

Manufactured and distributed by brebook publishing software (www.brebook.com)

Frank Bromilow

Butterflies of the Riviera

BUTTERFLIES
OF THE
RIVIERA

BY

FRANK BROMILOW

"I saw him run after a gilded butterfly; and when he caught it, he let it go again; and after it again; and over and over he comes, and up again, catched it again; or whether his fall enraged him, or how 'twas, he did so set his teeth and tear it, O, I warrant, how he mammocked it!"

SHAKESPEARE.
Coriolanus., Act I, scene 3.

A short account of the Rhopalocera of the Maritime Alps.

NICE
PRINTED BY P. CONSO & Co
11, Rue du Pont-Neuf, 11

—

1892

CONTENTS

	PAGE
Preface	1
Papilionidæ	5
Pieridæ	10
Lycænidæ	23
Erycinidæ	48
Libytheidæ	49
Apaturidæ	50
Nymphalidæ	53
Satyridæ	69
Hesperidæ	94
Bibliographical List	103
Index of Families	105
Index of Species, Varieties, and Synonyms	106
Appendix. — A List of Plants and their English names	110

EXPLANATION

OF THE

ABBREVIATIONS & TERMS USED

SIZE

″ used to express inches.
‴ lines ; a line being a twelfth part of an inch.

SEX

♂ means male.
♀   ″   female

OTHER TERMS USED

ab...............................	aberration.
f.-w.............................	fore-wing.
h.-w.............................	hind-wing.
u.-s.............................	under-side.
v. or var.......................	variety.

PREFACE

The present brief description of the butterflies of this district, was undertaken to supply a long-felt want amongst practical entomologists. No work of the kind has been attempted since the publication, nearly thirty years ago, of Millière's now scarce *Catalogue raisonné des Lépidoptères du département des Alpes-Maritimes*. This latter, though invaluable as far as it goes, is by no means comprehensive, and is often not reliable. Further; the taxonomy and nomenclature are obsolete. In some instances, species cited as belonging to the fauna of the department are found, on closer investigation to be erroneously considered so. This is, no doubt, due to the fact of that eminent lepidopterist having often accepted information on these points without having substantiated it.

As regards classification and naming. I have thought it best, in the present work, to follow that adopted by Dr O. Staudinger of Dresden, in his well-known *Catalogue*, as being the most complete and that generally used by European entomologists. Several species from the Pyrenees and Northern Italy are found in the Maritime

Alps ; but I have not included this area in the book, as the *whole* fauna of those places is not met with here.

The localities mentioned are those, for the most part, in which I myself have found certain insects, but it does not by any means follow that the species do not occur in other spots. I have purposely avoided the use of synonyms in dealing with the butterflies (except in a few cases), as not being within the scope of the present work ; but have appended a list of food-plants with their English names, at the end of the book.

The Butterflies of the Riviera is not primarily a descriptive manual, but merely a catalogue of species occurring in the district; descriptions, except in rare instances, where they are not usually to be found in the books, or in the case of some of the more interesting varieties, therefore, as well as tables for the determination of genera and species are omitted.

Some new matter will be found on the habits &c., of certain larvae not generally met with in previous treatises, as, for example, in the description of the early stages of *Erebia Neoridas*.

A special feature will be made in dealing with the early life-history of species.

The two former of the rudimentary stages,

viz., : — the egg and caterpillar state — being most necessary to an exhaustive study of the perfect insect.

Furthermore : there can be little doubt that a thorough knowledge of the ovum and larval periods, (especially the first of these, of which little has been written), would, in many instances, throw much light on the uncertain and often total disappearance of certain insects from favourite haunts.

Exception might perhaps be taken to the use of the singular, — ovum in the headings descriptive of eggs.

This plan is adopted in most of the works in dealing with the larvae, and therefore must be followed in the case of the eggs. It may perhaps seem an oddity to talk of the *egg* of a butterfly, whereas to say the *eggs*, is taken as a matter of course.

To show that grammatical accuracy is not sacrificed for the sake of effect, I may quote among instances, the description of the ova of *Pieris Rapae*. — " Ovum. — The *ova* of this species resemble a sugar-loaf, and *are* beautifully ribbed longitudinally ", &c., &c.

In conclusion ; I have to thank entomological friends who have, at any time, assisted me in the present undertaking, especially in regard to information, dates, &c., but, while gladly availing myself of these latter, I can by no means hold myself responsible for their authenticity or correctness.

I am indebted for much valuable information to my cousin, Edward Comerford Casey ; and my acknowledgments are also due to M. Thibon de Courtry, of Cannes.

Any modifications or suggestions will meet with consideration and, if deemed suitable, may perhaps find a place in a future edition.

F. B.

Nice, France.,
  April 1892.

BUTTERFLIES OF THE RIVIERA

Family 1. — PAPILIONIDÆ

Genus 1. — PAPILIO

P. Podalirius.
TIMES OF APPEARANCE. — April to September.
HABITAT. — Common everywhere as far north as Roquebillière ; rare at Saint-Martin-Vésubie.
LARVA. — On Almond, Sloe, Plum, Apple, Pear and Cherry, &c., in June and September.
Turns yellow when full-fed.
PUPA. — Chiefly on walls, which it resembles in colour.
VARIETIES.— v. **Undecimlineata** and v. **Zanclœus**.
In the first of these forms, the f.-w. have one or more extra bands of black, which are not present in the type.
HABITAT. — It is found in the same localities as the typical insect ; but is rare, being more strictly confined to North Africa. I am indebted to Herr R. Püngeler of Rhedyt, for information about this variety.
Zanclœus is an aberrant form of the second brood.

P. Alexanor.
TIMES OF APPEARANCE. — June to the end of July.

Habitat. — Saint-Martin-Vésubie, on the Route de Venanson ; and the valley of the Madone, extending as far south as La Bollène, though less plentifully.

Larva. — On *Seseli montanum* and other alpine *Umbelliferae*, in July and August.

Observation. — The ground colour of this larva is generally described as being green ; this is incorrect. During the four successive years in which I have collected caterpillars, (last summer 1891, I found seventy-one), I have never seen a single individual of this colour.

They are dirty whitish, with the usual bands and markings given in the works. I may here state that I have found eggs of the species, as early as July 18th, and a few stragglers of larvae, even as late as September 28th.

P. Machaon.

Times of Appearance. — May to the end of August.

Habitat. — Generally distributed ; but does not ascend to any great elevation in the mountains.

Ovum. — Oval, and of a pale green colour, but changes in a few days to steel-blue, and before the exit of the caterpillar, to black. From April to August.

Larva. — On *Daucus carota* (Wild Carrot), *Anethum fœniculum* (Fennel) and other *Umbelliferae*, from June to September.

The caterpillars of this species, when very young bear a close resemblance to those of *P. Alexanor* ; they however, differ from the former in having short spines, and are of a reddish colour.

Pupa. — Larger and rounder than that of the last ;

it is grey in colour, but sometimes green ; and is met with on rocks, walls palings and other similar situations.

VARIETY. — v. **Sphyrus**.
This form is smaller and darker than the type.

Genus 2. — THAIS

T. Polyxena.

TIME OF APPEARANCE. — April.
In forward seasons it is found in March.
I have seen or taken it on two successive seasons (1889-90), on April 1st and 9th respectively. I am informed on reliable authority, that it has been caught at Cannes, in fair abundance, though slightly worn, up to April 21st.

HABITAT. — Vence-Cagnes, near the mouth of the River Loup ; also at Cannes.
According to the late M. Bruyat, the *doyen* of local collectors, often quoted by Millière, *Thais* probably occurs at Levens. It frequents marshy ground, and is of short duration.

OVUM. — The eggs are round, shiny, and white with a distinct yellow tinge.
The ova in my collection are from a number, (thirty-six), deposited by a ♀, April 7th 1892, in the interior of a collecting-box, and were given to me.

VARIETIES. — v. **Ochracea**.
and v. **Cassandra**.

I have never met with these varieties, the specimens of this genus which I sent to Dr Staudinger, were certified to be the type *Polyxena*, though Millière claims that the typical form does not exist in the department.

T. Medesicaste.

TIMES OF APPEARANCE. — End of April, and May.

HABITAT. — L'Estérel and Trayas, near Cannes; Grasse ; also " on the heights of Cannet." — *Mil.*

On May 23rd 1890, several ♀ specimens among others, were taken on the hill-side at Trayas. They were all rather worn.

LARVA. — On *Aristolochia pistolochia*, in March and April.

OBSERVATION. — *Medesicaste* is now considered as specifically distinct from *Rumina*, of which it was formerly supposed to be a variety.

The Rev. Douglas C. Timins, who is acquainted with the larva of *Medesicaste*, describes it as specifically distinct from *Rumina*, on account of the caterpillar, which differs from that of the type.

The difference, however, seems to be chiefly one of coloration.

Genus 3. — PARNASSIUS

P. Apollo.

TIMES OF APPEARANCE. — June, July and August.

HABITAT. — Saint-Martin-Vésubie, and mountainous parts generally. Common.

LARVA. — On *Saxifrages* and *Crassulaceae*, in May, June and July.

I found a caterpillar, full grown, in the valley of the Boréon, not far from the Cascade (Italy), July 19th 1891.

It was discovered in the crevice of a rough stone wall. Five days later it began to pupate, spinning itself up amongst the leaves of a plant of *Saxifrage*, which I had previously placed in the breeding-cage for that purpose.

In another five days the pupa was finished. The chrysalid itself could easily be seen, between its rudimentary covering of web and leaves.

On July 27th of the same summer, it emerged from the chrysalis state.

P. Mnemosyne.

TIMES OF APPEARANCE. — June and July.

HABITAT. — According to the late A. Risso, Saint-Dalmas; Fenestre; the "Cinq Lacs" (Five Lakes); but I have never had any authentic account of its capture from entomologists, nor have I ever taken it myself.

LARVA. — On *Corydalis Halleri*, in April and May.

PUPA. — Somewhat resembles that of *Apollo*, spinning up among leaves.

Family 2. — PIERIDÆ

Genus 1. — APORIA

A. Crataegi.
TIMES OF APPEARANCE. — May and June.
HABITAT. — Common.
OVUM. — In clusters on the food-plant, in June.
The young larvae hatch in a period varying from ten to fourteen days.
LARVA.—Feeds in company on *Crataegus oxyacantha* (Hawthorn), Sloe, Cherry, and many other fruit trees.
PUPA. — Much resembles that of *P. Brassicae*, but is yellow, and the black spots are larger and more clearly defined. I found a chrysalis of this butterfly at Saint-Martin, by the road-side, on a dry stem of grass, June 12th 1891. The imago emerged eleven days later.

Genus 2. — PIERIS

P. Brassicæ.
TIMES OF APPEARANCE. — April to September, and sometimes later.
HABITAT. — Generally distributed.
OVUM. — " The eggs are laid in May, and again in July, sometimes singly and sometimes in little clusters, varying in number from four or five to a dozen. In shape they somewhat resemble a champagne bottle which has had the upper part of its neck knocked off.......... The attachment is by the base only, and the egg stands erect like a ninepin ; it has

twenty or twenty-two longitudinal ribs, and between thirty and forty most delicate lines, which pass over the ribs themselves, as well as the interstices between them ". — *E. Newman.*

LARVA. — On various *Cruciferae*, also on *Tropaeolums*, all the year round.

A fact has been communicated to me, with reference to the caterpillar of *Brassicae*, which is here worth chronicling. It has been observed in the act of laying eggs on *Capparis spinosa* (Caper), a plant belonging to a tropical order, distantly related to the *Cruciferae*.

PUPA.—Abundant on walls, palings and outhouses, &c.

P. Rapæ.

TIMES OF APPEARANCE. — April to October.

HABITAT. — Common everywhere; somewhat less abundant than the former.

OVUM.— The ova of this species resemble a sugarloaf, and are beautifully ribbed longitudinally, and delicately striated transversely, the number of ribs varying usually from ten to twelve. The striæ are considered inconstant; and are scarcely ever less than thirty. These eggs are attached by the base to the upper side of the leaf. They are found in April and May, and also in July and August. The young caterpillars are often observed eating the shell before quitting it.

LARVA. — On *Cruciferae*, in June and September.

PUPA. — Same kind of places as the last.

P. Napi.

TIMES OF APPEARANCE. — April to September.

Habitat. — Vallon Obscur and Mont Vinaigrier, Nice ; Vence-Cagnes, and many other places.
Not uncommon.

Ovum. — Conical, longitudinally ribbed, and striated transversely. The first brood occurs in April and May; the second, in July and August.

Larva. — On *Cruciferae* and *Resedaceae*, from June to September.

Varieties. — v. Napaeæ.
and   ab. Bryoniæ, ♀.

Habitat.—The former is found in the same localities as the type.

Bryoniae is a beautiful dark form of the female, found in mountainous districts.

Habitat. — It occurs at Saint-Martin-Vésubie, on the Chemin de Venanson ; also at the Cascade (Boréon).

P. Callidice.

Times of Appearance. — June to August, and even September.

Habitat. — Mt. Balme de la Freina, at Saint-Martin-Vésubie, at an elevation of 8000 feet, and over ; and Madone des Fenêtres near the " Lac ", among other localities.

Larva. — On *Arabis alpina* and other alpine *Cruciferae*, in August and the beginning of September.

Pupa. — The chrysalis passes the winter fastened to the rocks, the imago emerging in the following summer.

Observations. — Local in its habits ; but abundant where it occurs. The females of *Callidice* are considerably scarcer than the males. It may here be well to observe that this butterfly is somewhat difficult to capture, on account of its rapid flight.

A good plan, which I have always found effective, is to place oneself directly in the course of the insect, and so interrupt its further progress through the air.

P. Daplidice.

TIMES OF APPEARANCE. — From April to August, being double-brooded.

HABITAT. — Nice, in the Vallon Obscur, Vallon des Fleurs, &c.; Saint-Martin-Vésubie, on the Route de Venanson ; also on the " zig-zags ", on the ascent of the Balme de la Frema. Fairly common.

OVUM. — In April or May ; and again in August and September.

LARVA. — On *Reseda luteola* (Weld), Cabbage, and various *Cruciferae* and *Resedaceae*, in June and September.

VARIETY. — v. Bellidice.
Smaller than the type. Marginal band of f.-w. less extensive ; and powdered with white scales. U. S : f.-w. without the inner marginal spot in the ♂. H.-w., deeper green.

HABITAT. — Same as the type.

Genus 3. — ANTHOCARIS

A. Bella.

TIMES OF APPEARANCE. — March to June.
I have taken it sometimes, on March 1st.

HABITAT.— Mt. Vinaigrier and Vallon Obscur, Nice;

Cannes, &c.; and at Saint-Martin-Vésubie it is taken as high as the Cascade of the Boréon.

OVUM. — The ova are long, thickest in the centre and tapering to a point at each end, and, like all of the genus, ribbed longitudinally with grooves; they are shiny. When extruded, their colour is pale greenish-blue, which soon changes to deep orange inclining to red, and, before the exit of the young caterpillar, to lead colour, darkest at the apex. They are laid singly, attached by the base which is flattened, in an erect position on the buds or the stems of the buds of *Biscutella*, &c., there being sometimes as many as six or seven eggs on one plant.

They are found in April.

On April 19th this year, I collected twenty-six ova of the present species, together with larvæ. Two only, out of this quantity of eggs were bluish in colour.

The next day, several of them changed to a dark hue.

LARVA. — On *Biscutella didyma*, *B. Burseri* and other *Cruciferae*, from April to the end of June. I have met with very small caterpillars, as early as April 19th, in two different seasons (1890 and 1892), and as late as June 18th.

PUPA. — In May and of June. Those of the summer brood are capable of remaining as chrysalids for a period of two and even three years.

VARIETIES. — v. **Ausonia**.
and   v. **Simplonia**.

The former of these is a variety of the second brood, and is found in the same localities as the type.

Simpolonia corresponds to the *ab. Bryoniae* of *P. Napi*.

HABITAT. — It has been taken at or near Saint-Martin-Vésubie, on the Route de Venanson, Cascade, and other places, and is an alpine form of the species.

A. Tagis v. Bellezina.

TIME OF APPEARANCE. — April.
Some works say " March to May ".
HABITAT. — Millière quotes to the effect that it is " assez rare ".
LARVA. — On *Iberis pinnata*, in June and July.
OBSERVATION. — The type *Tagis* is not represented here ; it is only found in Portugal and Andalusia.

A. Cardamines.

TIMES OF APPEARANCE. — April, May and June.
HABITAT. — At Nice : in the Vallon Obscur, Mt. Vinaigrier, &c.; also at Vence-Cagnes and Cannes.
OVUM.— It has the same form as all those composing the genus ; and is glazed ; in colour, opal with a very slight yellowish tint, afterwards changing to orange-red if fertile,. and before the exit of the caterpillar to dull lead-colour, transparent at the tip.

It is laid singly, attached by the base which is flat, in an upright position on the peduncle (or flower-stalk) of the plant, sometimes in the very centre of the racemes, in which position it requires careful hunting for. Occasionally several eggs occur on one plant ; but never in the same position. Found from April to June. On April 22nd of this year, I watched a female ovipositing on the flower-heads of *Turritis glabra*. On examining a plant which I had just observed her to visit, I found an egg. On several subsequent occasions, I secured others. The larva emerged in nine days.

LARVA. — On *Cardamine pratense, C. impatiens, Turritis glabra*, and other *Cruciferae*, in July; hybernating in the chrysalis state.

VARIETIES. — Specimens are to be seen from time to time, in which the orange blotch occurs on only one of the f.-w., or only on the upper-side or under-side. Abnormities also occur having the whole ground colour canary-yellow.

A. Euphenoides.

TIMES OF APPEARANCE. — End of March to May.

It has been taken as early as March 22nd and 28th, in Nice.

The females, as is usual with most butterflies, emerge from their chrysalids about a fortnight later than the males; and are somewhat rare.

HABITAT. — Vallon Obscur, Mt. Vinaigrier and gorge of Saint-André, Nice; rarer at Cannes; also at Saint-Martin-Vésubie, where it is never very common.

It is interesting to note that it is to be taken even as high as the Boréon bridge, over the torrent near Saint-Martin. The specimens from the alpine parts strangely enough appear larger than those from the coast.

OVUM.— The ova are shaped like those of *A. Belia;* in colour pale yellow. They are deposited in a vertical position on the young buds of the food plant, being found in May.

LARVA. — On *Biscutella didyma, B. Burseri* and other kinds of *Cruciferae*, in June and July, according to the altitude.

In the summer of 1890 (from July 3rd to 5th), I collected in the mountains altogether sixteen caterpillars, nearly all full-fed. They were all found on a tall alpine crucifer, probably *Sisymbrium polyceratium*, sometimes as many as five on one plant.

The imagines came out in the following spring, (from May 3rd onwards).

PUPA. — Can vary in colour from light drab or greyish buff bordered at the sides with a deeper shade, and with dark dorsal line, to light green. These chrysalids are more arched than those of the preceding species. Out of eight pupae of the normal colour only one was green.

The imago (a male) which emerged from this latter, differed in no way from the others.

OBSERVATION. — Imagines are variable in size. One specimen which I possess, measures only 1" 3‴ from the tip to tip of each fore-wing.

The larvae of *Euphenoides* are easily reared with care from the eggs, on the air-tight principle of the corked bottle.

The food-plant, which remains fresh for a considerable time, must not be allowed to get mouldy, and the bottle must never be exposed to the direct rays of the sun.

Care must be taken not to allow moisture to collect on the sides of this too readily heat conducting larvarium.

I may add, that I have successfully experimented with the larvae of *R. Cleopatra* and *C. Pamphilus*, from the ova.

Euphenoides is known by the French, as the
" Gloire de Provence ". This species and the closely
allied *A. Eupheno* from North Africa, were long
confounded ; to avoid confusion then, Dr Staudinger
proposed the name of *Euphenoides* of the present
species.

Genus 4. — LEUCOPHASIA

L. Sinapis.

TIMES OF APPEARANCE. — April and August.

HABITAT. — Common. Found in shady spots.

LARVA. — On *Vicia cracca, Lotus, Lathyrus* and
other plants of the order *Leguminosae,* in June and
September, the insect being double-brooded.

VARIETIES. — v. **Erysimi.**
             v. **Lathyri.**
and   v. **Diniensis.**

The latter variety is rather less common than the
former in the district.

L. Duponchell.

TIMES OF APPEARANCE. — May to August.

HABITAT. — I have no account of its capture in the
department ; but, as it is stated in the entomological
works as belonging to South-Eastern France, I insert
it herewith.

LARVA. — Not described.

OBSERVATION. — The species was first described by
Duponchel, in 1832.

Genus 5. — COLIAS

C. Palaeno.

TIMES OF APPEARANCE. — July and August.

HABITAT. — According to Pierre Millière, "All the heights of the department, from 1.800 mètres (5904 feet) to 2.000 mètres (6560 feet) where type and variety are not rare. Ch.? "

LARVA. — On *Vaccinium uliginosum* and *Coronilla*, in May.

The female of *Palaeno*, like most of the genus is dimorphic, but departs from the general rule in having the normal form white. There is, however, a yellow form which is found at a greater altitude than the type, namely the

VARIETY. — *ab.* Werdandi, *H. S.*

OBSERVATION. — Staudinger, like Millière gives a v. *Europomene.*, Och.

The former also enumerates an *ab. Werdandi* amongs the varieties of the type.

Is, then, the *var. Europomene* of Millière's Catalogue identical with Staudinger's *Werdandi* of H. S., or is *Europomene* separate ?

C. Phicomone.

TIMES OF APPEARANCE. — July and August.

HABITAT — Mt. Colmiane, Mt. Balme de la Frema ; Madone des Fenêtres (Fenestres) ; also heights of Berthemont, at an altitude of never less than 5000 feet.

I observed a single specimen of the ♀, on the Colmiane, as late as October 14th, one year.

LARVA.— On different kinds of *Leguminosae*, chiefly of the genus *Vicia*.

C. Hyale.

TIMES OF APPEARANCE. — From July to the end of September, and again in the spring after hybernation.

HABITAT. — Generally distributed.

OVUM. — The eggs are laid in the spring by hybernated females.

LARVA. — On *Medicago, Coronilla varia* and other *Leguminosae*, in June and July.

OBSERVATION. — Hybrids of this species and the next occur ; specimens possessing the characters of each being met with.

C. Edusa.

TIMES OF APPEARANCE. — May and June, and from August until November.

HABITAT. — Common.

OVUM. — According to Newman, " They are placed in an erect position on the upper side of the leaf, and are shaped much like a ninepin, somewhat tapering towards both ends, and decidedly pointed at the tip ; their colour, when extruded, is pale yellow, but they gradually assume a darker hue, and finally become tinged with pink." They may be met with in the spring.

LARVA.— On *Medicago lupulina* and various species of *Trifolium*, in June and July.

VARIETY. — ab. Helice, ♀.

Somewhat scarce. Intermediate forms are of constant occurrence.

Genus 6. — RHODOCERA

R. Rhamni.
TIMES OF APPEARANCE. — From the end of July to October, and in the spring after hybernation.

HABITAT. — Saint-Martin-Vésubie, on the Chemin de Venanson (though I am not quite sure of its identity), where it is rare ; it is, however, fairly common at the Lac de la Madone, flying wildly across the heights, at an altitude of 7500 feet. Not found on the coast.

OVUM. — The eggs are deposited singly on the twigs of the food-plant by hybernated females, after hybernation, about the middle of April.

LARVA. — On *Rhamnus frangula*, *R. catharticus* and *Prunus spinosa* (Blackthorn), in May, and is full-fed by the end of June.

OBSERVATION. — *Rhamni* is essentially a native of Northern and Central Europe. It is, however, enumerated in all the local faunas.

R. Farinosa.
TIMES OF APPEARANCE. — From the end of July to October, and in the spring after hybernaton.

HABITAT. — Same as the last, of which it used to be considered a form.

LARVA. — Unknown.

R. Cleopatra.
TIMES OF APPEARANCE. — April and May, and again in July ; but the second brood is much less abundant than the spring one.

HABITAT. — Common everywhere ; rare at Saint-Martin-Vésubie.

OVUM. — From May to June.

The eggs are laid on the under surface of the terminal shoots of the food-plant, and the larva emerges within a week from the time of having been deposited.

Out of a large number of ova (more than twenty), nearly all yielded caterpillars which fed up rapidly.

LARVA. — On *Rhamnus alpinus* and other species of Buckthorn, in May and June. The sole caterpillar which I reserved out of the above number, took exactly four weeks and a day (May 19th to June 16th), from the time it was hatched till the date when the larva changed to a chrysalis.

It remained in the pupal state three weeks — June 16th to July 6th — at the end of which period one evening at 7-30, the imago came forth. The time thus occupied, — from the birth of the caterpillar to the exit of the butterfly being seven weeks and one day.

PUPA. — Is found in July.

The chrysalid which I have in my collection is fastened to a twig of the plant on which the larva had formerly subsisted.

OBSERVATION. — Many entomologists consider this to be a variety of the last ; but it is difficult to see on what grounds.

Family 3. — LYCÆNIDÆ

Genus 1. — THECLA

T. Betulæ.

TIMES OF APPEARANCE. — From the end of July to the middle of September.

HABITAT. — Nice, in the Vallon Obscur ; also at Saint-Martin-Vésubie, on the Chemin de Venanson and the valley of the Madone, as well as various other spots in the vicinity.

Not uncommon in the autumn.

OVUM. — The eggs are laid in September, on the twigs of the food-plant.

" The egg is a depressed sphere, and white."— *Newman*. The caterpillar emerges in the spring, and is full-fed by June.

LARVA. — On birch, blackthorn and the common plum also, according to Millière, on poplar and hazel ; from June to August.

On August 5th 1890, I received a larva of *Betulae*, which immediately began to pupate.

The imago appeared in a week.

Last season (1891),on June 20th and 23rd, I found two caterpillars, one half-grown, the other full-fed, on a bush of *Prunus*, off the road which leads to the village of Venanson.

The large one began to pupate, eleven days later.

PUPA. — It is not attached by silken threads, thus resembling the chrysalis of *T. Quercûs*, which also does not attach itself by the head and tail and is by some authors placed, with the present species, in the genus *Zephyrus*, Dalm.

T. Spini.

TIMES OF APPEARANCE. — May and June.

HABITAT. — Saint-Martin-Vésubie, on the Route de Venanson ; also in the valley of the Madone.

It has been taken near the summit of the Balme de la Frema, at an altitude of about 7500 feet. Common.

LARVA. — On *Prunus spinosa* (Sloe) ; *Crataegus oxyacantha* (Hawthorn). I have always found it on *Rhamnus catharticus* (Common Buckthorn), though it is not stated in the works as living on this plant. Millière also gives wild rose (rosier sauvage). Found in June.

The caterpillars may be obtained by beating the plants on which they live.

Of the eighty-one larvae I collected, in the summer of 1891 (from June 14th to 24th), nearly every one succeeded.

PUPA. — Much resembles that of *Spini*.

It is brown. The first chrysalis of those I collected, was formed June 25th; the last one was finished on July 23rd.

VARIETIES. — v. **Lynceus**.

Upper surface with large yellow spots.

Another form, which is rather an accidental aberration than a fully established variety, has the white bands of the under side, especially on the h.-w., considerably enlarged.

I have here to mention, what is apparently a curious hybrid of *T. Spini* and *Ilicis*, specimens of which I now possess, but can find no mention of it in the books.

They were obtained from larvae, (presumably of *Spini*), collected last summer, (1891). The wings have the same expanse as *Spini*, and the upper surface of the f.-w. resembles that of *T. Spini*, but has the dull orange patch on the f.-w., like *Ilicis* ; and the h.-w. have *large* yellowish spots at the anal angle. In the ♀, there are five of these graduating in size, of a lighter colour than the ♂, instead of one.

The u.-s. of all the wings is identical with that of *Spini*, having the ample clearly defined white zig-zag lines, &c.

It has the large blue spot at the anal angle of the. h.-w.

There are also faint traces of yellow spots on the hind-margin of the f.-w.

I may add that I only got two of these remarkable varieties out of eighty-one larvae.

T. W. — Album.

TIMES OF APPEARANCE. — July and August.

HABITAT. — Nice, at Saint-Barthélemy, &c., and at Cannes. A ♀ specimen was captured on a plant of marguerite daisies in the first mentioned locality, on June 10th 1890. The species had been taken in the same spot, at an almost identical date in the preceding season.

It is not very common in Nice owing, I suppose to the scarcity of its food-plant, in the larval state, in the neighbourhood.

OVUM.— On the twigs of the elm, in July and August.

LARVA.— On *Ulmus campestris* (Common Elm) and *U. montana* (Wych Elm), from whence it may be obtained by beating, after hybernation at the end of May and the beginning of June.
Turns brown when full-grown.
PUPA. — Attached to the stems of the food-plant.

T. Pruni.
TIME OF APPEARANCE. — June.
HABITAT. — ?
OVUM. — The eggs are laid in the summer and remain all the winter, hatching in the following spring.
LARVA. — On *Prunus spinosa*, oak and other trees, in May.

T. Ilicis ab. Cerri ♀,
and   v. Æsculi.
TIMES OF APPEARANCE. — May, June and September.
HABITAT. — Saint-Martin-Vésubie and many other places. In the former locality it is found on the Route de Venanson, among or near oak trees.

I captured a very fresh specimen of *Cerri*, on July 5th 1890, in the last mentioned spot. *Æsculi* is found in this place also.

Three very worn specimens intermediate between the type and ab. *Cerri*, were taken on July 19th 1891.

OBSERVATION. — The typical *Ilicis* does not exist in the South of France or Spain.

T. Acaciæ.
TIMES OF APPEARANCE. — June and July.
HABITAT. — Rare.

LARVA. — On *Prunus communis* (sloe) " preferring the smallest and most depauperated bushes ", *(Hof)*, in June.

T. Ledereri.

TIME OF APPEARANCE. — June.

HABITAT. — Route de Venanson, at Saint-Martin-Vésubie ? Rare. Any really authentic accounts of the capture of this *Thecla* in the department, would be of value to the lepidopterological fauna. It is usually considered as belonging to Armenia and the Trans-Caucasus.

LARVA. — Unknown.

T. Roboris.

TIMES OF APPEARANCE. — May and June.

HABITAT.— Saint-Martin-Vésubie, in the same localities as *T. Quercûs*. It is somewhat rare, four or five individuals only, being captured in the course of a season by entomologists.

LARVA. — " Dull brown, with a black dorsal streak bordered with obscure yellow markings." (V. G.) " On oak ? " (*Kirby, Man. Eur. But.*, p. 87), and ash *(Fraxinus)*.

OBSERVATION. — Some authors constitute *Roboris* as a separate species and place it in the genus *Laeosopis* (Ram), but as it is included in the genus *Thecla* by Dr Staudinger, I have thought it best to follow his arrangement.

The eyes of this species are not hairy as in *Thecla*. The hind-margins of the h.-w. are not scalloped near the anal angle, and the u.-s. does not show the light coloured streaks, but has rows of black spots along the hind-margins.

T. Quercûs.

TIMES OF APPEARANCE.— July and August.

I took a ♀ of this species very fresh, on July 30th 1891.

HABITAT. — Saint-Martin-Vésubie, on the high-road to Nice about two miles from the village, in a copse of oak trees off the road ; also, Route de Venanson.

Its habit of frequenting oak woods is well known, hovering over the tops of the trees, and settling on the leaves.

OVUM. — On the twigs of oak, in July.

LARVA. — On *Quercus robur* (Common Oak), in May and June.

Stainton says " I find the statement that the larva of this species frequently undergoes its transformations below the surface of the earth, perfectly substantiated. Carnivorous in captivity.

PUPA. — The caterpillar on assuming the chrysalis state, is said by the most accurate observers not to attach itself by the tail or by a silken belt, thus resembling the pupa of *Thecla Betulae*, with which species the present one is placed in the genus *Zephyrus* by many modern entomologists.

T. Rubi.

TIMES OF APPEARANCE.— April, May and August.

HABITAT. — Common everywhere.

OVUM. — Early in June.

LARVA. — On the flower buds of *Rubus* (Bramble), *Genista* and various Papilionaceous plants. It is full-fed by the beginning of July.

Pupa. — The Rev. Joseph Green mentions that he has found this chrysalis under moss, on an old tree trunk.

Genus 2. — THESTOR

T. Ballus.
Times of Appearance. — End of March and beginning of April.
Habitat. — " It has been taken from time to time, on the waste land of Vallauris, at the beginning of April."— *Mil.*
Larva. — On *Lotus hispidus*, in May.

Genus 3. — POLYOMMATUS

P. Virgaureœ.
Times of Appearance. — May and August.
Habitat. — Saint-Martin-Vésubie, Thorenc, &c., where it is always abundant.
Larva. — On *Solidago virgaureae*, (Golden Rod) and various species of *Rumex*, in June and September.

P. Thersamon v. Omphale.
Time of Appearance. — July.
Habitat.— I quote Millière., " Vallée de Lantosque, hauteurs de 1,000 mètres (3280 feet), to 1,500 mètres, (4920 feet), où elle se montre partout et où cette variété constante semble remplacer le type. Ch.? "
Larva. — Unknown.
Observation. — I may mention that Dr Lang, (*But. Eur.*, vol. I., p. 138), gives the habitat of this variety as Asia Minor.

P. Hippothoë.

TIMES OF APPEARANCE. — June to September.

HABITAT. — Saint-Martin-Vésubie in the valley of the Madone, also at the Madone des Fenêtres, not far from the hotel.
It is not uncommon at this altitude.

OVUM. — In August.

LARVA.— On *Rumex hydrolapathum* and *R. acetosa*, in June.

VARIETIES. — v. Confluens and v. Eurybia.

HABITAT. — Saint-Martin-Vésubie and the valley of the Madone, in fields and moist places. Rather wider distribution than the type.

P. Gordius.

TIMES OF APPEARANCE. — June to August.

HABITAT.— Saint-Martin-Vésubie on the Route de Venanson, where it is always common in the full sun; it also occurs in the valley of the Madone, and is to be met with at a height of 7000 to 7500 feet; and at Cimiez, Nice, (A. Risso).

LARVA. — Unknown.

P. Dorilis.

TIMES OF APPEARANCE. — The greater part of the year, from early spring to late autumn.

HABITAT.— Saint-Martin-Vésubie, especially on the Chemin de Venanson, in hot sunny spots, &c.

LARVA. — On *Rumex acetosa* and *Cytisus scoparia*, in April and May.

There are three or four broods in the year.

VARIETY. — v. Subalpina.

HABITAT. — Madone des Fenêtres near Saint-Martin-Vésubie, at a height of 6000 feet and over; also Mt. Balme de la Frema.

This very dark variety, which resembles the *v. Simplonia* of *Anthocaris Belia*, is usually found at a greater elevation than the type.

P. Phlæas.

TIMES OF APPEARANCE. — Throughout the greater part of the year, there being several broods.

I have taken it in Nice, as early as the end of February.

HABITAT. — Common everywhere.

LARVA. — On various species of *Rumex*, in May, July and September.

VARIETIES. — v. Schmidtii.
and   v. Eleus.

The following description of *Schmidtii* is taken from Lang.,vol. I, p. 96 , I can find no other satisfactory mention of it in the works I have consulted.

It will, no doubt, enable collectors who may be so fortunate as to chance to find this very scarce variety in identifying it. " In this form, all those portions of the wing that are normally copper-coloured are brilliant shining white."

HABITAT. — " It is found most commonly in the southern districts of the territory inhabited by *P. Phlaeas*, but it occasionally occurs in the more northern parts ". . . . .

Eleus is darker than the type *Phlaeas*

It is a southern variety.

Habitat.— Found at Nice, Cannes, Saint-Martin-Vésubie, &c., in the same localities as the type.

Genus 4. — LYCÆNA

L. Bœtica.

Times of Appearance. — August, September, and October.

Habitat. — I know of no special locality where it is to be found ; but on October 8th 1888, I took a superb ♀ specimen of the insect, at Ray, near Nice. It is rather scarce.

It is found at Cannes, where it has been stated to occur up to December.

Ovum. — " The eggs are laid in the autumn, on the twigs of the plants, the newly emerged larva entering the young pods in the following summer ; when it is fully grown, it undergoes its pupation on the stems, or in the leaves."

Larva.— On *Colutea arborescens* and *Pisum sativum* (common garden pea), in June and July.

Observation. — It is not unlikely that this species may occur at Lantosque, near the high-road to Nice, as plants of the *Colutea* grow there.

L. Telicanus.

Times of Appearance. — July to October.

Millière states from February. Stragglers in some seasons may be taken, rather worn, as late as the beginning of November.

Habitat. — Nice, in the Vallon Obscur, Vallon des Fleurs, and the Valley of the Mantega; it occurs also at Saint-Martin-Vésubie on the high-road, though less abundantly than at the coast.

On September 24th 1889, I took six ragged specimens, all males, in the Vallon Obscur.

They were hovering over a bramble bush. They seem to have a partiality for dry torrent beds, settling on a large yellow composite, *Inula graveolens* which grows in these kind of spots.

The females are much scarcer than the males.

Larva. — On *Lythrum salicaria* (Purple loose-strife), on the flowers of which it feeds; also on *Calluna* (Ling), and probably several other low-growing plants, in August and September.

L. Aegon.

Times of Appearance. — May to August.

Habitat. — Saint-Martin-Vésubie, &c., where it is common.

Ovum. — In form circular; white " flattened and depressed in the centre both above and below, ribbed and beaded boldly at the sides, and from thence more finely by degrees to the centre.

The egg does not change colour, but retains its pure dead-white appearance even after the exit of the caterpillar; a small hole, showing like a black spot on the side of the shell, alone betraying the escape of the little creature." — C. G. Barrett, in Newman's *British Butterflies.*, volume I., page 119.

Larva. — On *Genista*, *Vicia*, and *Colutea*. Millière states *Ulex* ; in May and June.

Variety. — ab. **Argyrognomon** ♀. *(Stgr.)*
Usually stated in the books as a variety of *L. Argus.*

L. Argus.

Times of Appearance. — May to August.

Habitat. — I took two ♂ and two ♀ very fresh, besides others seen, on August 11th 1890. One of the ♀ was suffused with blue, but, according to Staudinger, was not the variety *Argyrognomon* of authors.

They were caught on the summit of Mt. Balme de la Frema, at an altitude of 8000 feet.

I have never taken it at a lower elevation.

Larva. — On various species of *Genista,* and on *Melilotus officinalis,* in May.

L. Orion.

Times of Appearance. — May to the end of July.

Habitat. — Levens, twenty-two kilomètres from Nice.

I took several specimens in good condition, in the gorge of Saint-André, near Nice, on June 9th 1891.

Larva. — On *Sedum telephium,* in July.

L. Baton.

Times of Appearance. — April to August, on the coast; May to August in elevated districts.

I have taken it on two successive seasons, (1889-90), as early as April 18th, and March 26th.

Habitat.— Mt. Vinaigrier, Nice; and is very scarce at Saint-Martin-Vésubie.

Larva. — (Of *v. Panoptes*).

Millière thus describes the caterpillar : —

" It is green, inclining to olive ; the head is black and retractile. There is a broad dorsal line of pink, bordered on each side by a narrow stripe of light yellow. In a line with the stigmata is a brilliant white stripe, the stigmata themselves being whitish.

" The ventral surface is green, but duller than the back and sides ; the legs *(pattes écailleuses)* are brown; the claspers *(pattes membraneuses)* are green.

" It feeds on *Thymus vulgaris*.

" The egg is hatched when the thyme is in full flower, and its growth is rapid, the pupa being formed by the first week in June.

" The pupa is ovoid, short, and slightly tapering at the extremities ; its surface is smooth, clay-coloured, the wing-cases being tinged with green." *Lg. But. Eur.* vol. I., p. 110.

He states it as occurring at Hyères, Cannes, and other places on the Mediterranean.

I may add that the two specimens of *Baton*, caught in Nice, which I sent to Dr Staudinger, several years ago, to be correctly designated, were stated by him to be the *Baton* type.

L. Lysimon.
TIME OF APPEARANCE. — July.

HABITAT. — Stated in the larger works as occurring in the South of France ; but I can find no record of its existence in the district, in local books on the butterflies.

LARVA. — Unknown.

L. Orbitulus.
TIME OF APPEARANCE. — July.

Habitat. — " Vallée de Lantosque ; pentes méridionales qui y aboutissent. Ch."— *Mil.*

L. Astrarche.

Times of Appearance. — April to October, there being a succession of broods in the year.

The individuals of the spring brood are larger and lighter than those of the later ones.

Habitat. — Vallon Obscur, Nice ; Saint-Martin-Vésubie, and other places.

Ovum. — Greenish white, changing in ten days to pure white, and having on its upper side a large kidney-shaped hole after the escape of the young larva. These eggs are laid on the under-side of the leaf of the food-plant ; and are found in August. — Adapted from *The Natural History of British Butterflies,* by Edward Newman F. L. S., F. Z. S., p. 124.

Larva. — On *Erodium cicutarium* (Stork-bill).

Pupa. — Spun up among the leaves of *Erodium* and *Artemesia.*

Variety. — v. Allous.

A varietal form of the summer brood.

L. Icarus.

Times of Appearance. — From May to September. There are several broods in the year.

Habitat. — Very common everywhere.

Ovum. — The eggs, which are round, smooth, and considerably flattened at the extremities, are pale bluish-green in colour.

They are laid on the buds of the food-plant.

I took a number of ova on a plant of *Ononis spinosa*, (Rest-Harrow), on August 1st 1891.

OBSERVATION. — It is a good plan when eggs of any given species are desired, to watch the parent female as she flies hither and thither, depositing ova. The portion of the plant on which the eggs are laid, can thus be easily secured.

Another plan, is to incarcerate an impregnated female in a darkened box, but which partially admits the rays of the sun. The interior can be loosely lined with leno or tissue paper, on which the insect can deposit her eggs, which can then be clipped off, if desired.

It is best to regale the insect thus imprisoned, with a sirup of sugar and water, once or twice daily. When the butterfly is required to partake of this fare, place the nectar before it, and blow her gently in its direction, when she will immediately unfold her proboscis and feed. Of course, when the female has deposited her complete stock of eggs or as many as are wanted, she can then be allowed to escape into the air, again.

I have always found this plan to succeed perfectly. This system, of course, applies to all species; though some are more difficult of treatment than others.

LARVA. — On *Ononis spinosa*, *Genista*, Grass and Clover, especially the former of these, in April, July and August.

VARIETIES, &c.,— v. Icarinus.

HABITAT. — Same localities as the type.

There is also a beautiful aberration of the ♀, in which all the wings are suffused with the blue of the ♂, thus answering to the *var. Ceronus* of *L. Bellargus*.

HABITAT. — Same as the type. It has been found, among other places, in the Vallon Obscur, Nice; and the Route de Venanson, at Saint-Martin-Vésubie. The coast specimens are usually finer than those from the alps. It is probably this form which is described by D*r* Staudinger as *ab. Caerulea.* This aberration is not very abundant. Intermediate forms are not rare.

L. Eumedon.

TIMES OF APPEARANCE. — July and August.

HABITAT.— Madone des Fenêtres, near Saint-Martin-Vésubie, about a quarter of a mile below the hotel.

LARVA. — On *Geranium pratense* (Blue Meadow Crane's-bill) and *G. purpureum* (Crimson Crane's-bill).,— *Hofm.*

L. Amanda.

TIMES OF APPEARANCE. — June to August.

HABITAT. — Saint-Martin-Vésubie, on the Chemin de Venanson, and at the Cascade of the Borréon, near Saint-Martin.

LARVA. — Unknown.

OBSERVATION. — Not very common.

L. Escheri.

TIMES OF APPEARANCE. — May to July.

HABITAT. — Nice, in the Vallon Obscur, &c., where it is not uncommon ; also Saint-Martin-Vésubie, on the Chemin de Venanson.

The female is rather less common.

I have a ♀ of this species, whose wings, front and hind, are suffused with blue ; I have seen no mention of it in the books, though it is well known that all the females of the *Lycaenidae* are subject to dimorphism.

L. Bellargus.

TIMES OF APPEARANCE. — From May, to the middle of September, being double-brooded.

HABITAT. — Vallon Obscur, Nice ; Chemin de Venanson, and the road leading to the Cascade, near Saint-Martin-Vésubie, &c. Its preference for chalky and limestone districts is well known. Like many of the genus, it is fond of settling on moist ground, near water. Common.

LARVA. — On *Lotus, Hippocrepis, Vicia,* and other kinds of *Leguminosae,* in May and June.

VARIETIES. — ab. Cinnus
and ab. Ceronus.

HABITATS. — Same as the type.

OBSERVATION. — " Hubner considered as belonging to the male *Ceronus,* those specimens of that sex which have a row of black dots on the hind-wings."— *Lg.*

L. Corydon.

TIMES OF APPEARANCE. — May to September.

HABITAT. — Generally distributed. It has the same habits as the preceding species.

LARVA. — On *Papilionaceae,* in May and June.

OBSERVATION.— It is somewhat difficult to distinguish between females of this and the preceding species, owing to their great similarity.

A point of difference, however, to be noted, is that in *Bellargus* the fringes of the wings are black and white ; while in *Corydon* they are white, spotted with black more distinctly than in *Bellargus.* Moreover, the undersides of the wings in *L. Corydon,* are similar to *Bellargus,* but the three basal spots are separated from the central row on the h.-w., so as not to form a regular curve round the discoidal spot.

L. Hylas.
TIMES OF APPEARANCE. — May to August.
HABITAT. — Saint-Martin-Vésubie, on the Chemin de Venanson ; and the Vallon Obscur, Nice. Not very common.
LARVA. — On the flowers of *Melilotus officinalis*, in May and August.

L. Meleager.
TIMES OF APPEARANCE. — May to July.
HABITAT. — Saint-Martin-Vésubie, on the Route de Venanson., &c.
LARVA. — Unknown.
VARIETY. — ab. **Stevenii**.
Same localities as the type. Rather uncommon.

L. Admetus v. Ripartii.
TIMES OF APPEARANCE. — June and July.
HABITAT. — ? It is only found on " the southern slopes of the Alps." *Lg.*

L. Dolus.
Lefeborei., Godt.
Mithridates., Stg.
TIMES OF APPEARANCE. — June to August.
HABITAT. — Not very common.
LARVA. — On *Onobrychis sativa*, in May.
OBSERVATION. — I cannot find the species known under these names, in Staudinger's *List* ; it is, however, probably *Mithridates*, which in order comes

between L. *Admetus* v. *Ripartii* and L. *Menaclas*, as *Dolus* does.

L. Menaclas.
TIMES OF APPEARANCE. — June to August.
HABITAT. — Same as the last.
LARVA. — Unknown.
OBSERVATION. — Formerly supposed to be a variety of *Dolus*. Dr Staudinger gives it specific rank.

L. Damon.
TIMES OF APPEARANCE. — June to August.
HABITAT. — Saint-Martin-Vésubie, on the Chemin de Venanson, ascending even as high as the summit of the Balme de la Frema.
LARVA. — On *Onobrychis sativa* and *supinus*, in May and June.
OBSERVATION. — It is rather local ; but common where it occurs. Its habit of frequenting saintfoin fields has been noticed.

L. Donzelii.
TIMES OF APPEARANCE. — June and July.
HABITAT. — Saint-Martin-Vésubie, in the valley of the Boréon. It is rather rare.
LARVA. — Unknown.

L. Argiolus.
TIMES OF APPEARANCE. — April to August, being double-brooded.
HABITAT. — Vallon Obscur, Nice, where it is always common ; rare at Saint-Martin-Vésubie.

I have observed it at this latter locality, near the torrent, which passes by the village.

OBSERVATION.— Its habit is to hover over the bushes, and the tops of the trees.

LARVA.— On the flowers of *Ilex* (Holly), *Hedera* (Ivy), *Rhamnus* (Buckthorn) and *Dorycnium*, in June, and again in the autumn.

L. Sebrus.

TIMES OF APPEARANCE. — May to July.

HABITAT. — Elevated hills in the neighbourhood of Grasse.

LARVA. — Unknown.

L. Minima.

TIMES OF APPEARANCE. — May to August.

HABITAT. — Saint-Martin-Vésubie, and many other places, where it is abundant, especially near damp spots and streams; rarer at Nice; it is also found at the Cascade of the Boréon and at the Madone, near Saint-Martin-Vésubie.

OVUM. — In colour glaucous; they are reticulated, and the meshes stand out in relief, rhomboidal, and knotted at the junction of their angles.

These eggs are laid singly, between the downy calyces of the flower-heads of *Anthyllis*, &c., in June. — Condensed from *Newman*.

LARVA. — On *Anthyllis vulneraria, Coronilla varia, Astragalus*, and several kinds of vetches, in June and August.

VARIETY. — v. **Lorquinii.**

Found in the same places as the type.

It is probably a distinct species.

OBSERVATION. — *Minima* is very variable; some specimens, specially from Northern Europe, measuring only half-an-inch, while others extend to an inch and sometimes more.

L. Semiargus.
TIMES OF APPEARANCE. — May to July.

HABITAT. — Saint-Martin-Vésubie, " Cascade ", &c., &c., where it is common, especially in fields, and near water.

OVUM. — Small, shiny, and round ; in colour they are white. The ♀ deposits a string of eggs, freely, even when impaled with the collector's pin.

LARVA. — In the flower-heads of *Armeria vulgaris* (Z), and *Anthyllis vulueraria*, (As).

L. Cœlestina.
TIMES OF APPEARANCE. — June and July.

HABITAT. — It is mentioned in Millière's work thus : " Juillet. Bords de la haute Vésubie et du Boréon."

LARVA. — Unknown.

OBSERVATION. — According to the above-quoted author, *Caelestina* is new to the entomological fauna of France. It is generally stated as occurring in Turkey, and the South-East of Russia (principally Sarepta).

L. Cyllarus.
TIMES OE APPEARANCE. — May, to the end of August.

HABITAT. — Nice, in the Vallon Obscur, &c., also at Saint-Martin-Vésubie, though less commonly.

LARVA. — On *Medicago*, *Onobrychis*, and several other kinds of *Leguminosae*, in June and July.

VARIETY. — Millière figures a variety which has the characters of *Cyllarus* and *Melanops*.

He says, "If this variety is not a distinct species, it might well be a variety of the two *Lycaenae*."

L. Melanops.

TIMES OF APPEARANCE. — April and May.

HABITAT AND LARVA.— It appears in May, and flies in the localities where the *Dorycnium decumbens* occurs. It is on this plant that the larva feeds, in June."—*Mil.*

Found in Nice, in the Vallon Obscur; also at Cannes and Thoreno., &c.

The caterpillar also lives on several other species of *Leguminosae*, till as late as July.

OBSERVATION. — The insect remains in the lethargic state, for more than ten months.

VARIETY. — v. **Marchandii**.

The spots on the u.-s. of the h.-w., are not ocellated, like the var. *Cinnus of Bellargus*.

Met with in the same localities as the typical form.

L. Iolas.

TIMES OF APPEARANCE. — June and July.

HABITAT. — I am not aware of any particular spot where it occurs.

LARVA. — On the pods of *Colutea arborescens*.

TIME OF APPEARANCE. — The time does not seem to be stated in the books; it probably appears in May.

L. Alcon.

TIMES OF APPEARANCE. — July and August.

HABITAT. — I have no account of its capture here; it is described as occurring in Southern Europe.

LARVA. — Unknown.

OBSERVATION. — A local species, occurring on moorland meadows.

L. Arion.

TIMES OF APPEARANCE.— From the end of May to the middle of July.

HABITAT. — Vallon Obscur, Nice ; Saint-Martin-Vésubie, on the Route de Venanson, &c., also at the Madone des Fenêtres.

OVUM. — It is spheroid, much depressed at the north pole, and concave at the south pole, where it is very slightly attached to the hairs of the calyx of the Thyme. The surface of the egg is reticulated. Its colour and texture much resembles white porcelain, with the slightest possible tint of green. — From *Newman*.

According to the same authority they are laid either singly, or in groups varying in number from two to six.

The young caterpillar, on quitting the egg, consumes a considerable portion of the shell.

LARVA. — It has never been observed in its full-grown state ; but has been described when thirteen days old (May 4th to 16th), as being of a dirty pink colour, the head brown and shiny, the dorsal line rust-colour.

It was reared by Mr Porritt of Huddersfield (England), on Wild Thyme *(Thymus)*, on the flowers of which it feeds, from May to July.

VARIETY. — v. **Cyanecula.**, *Ev. Bull. Mosc ; H. S.* 593-4.

Wings rather lighter above. U. S.: h.-w. have the

ground colour greenish-blue throughout the whole area between the base and the hind-marginal row of black spots. Rare.

OBSERVATION. — On June 23rd 1890, I caught four specimens of the typical *Arion*, in the first-mentioned locality, (one of them was a male and three were females). They were all fresh except one, a ♀.

They were captured in a little field, on the west side of the Vallon near the entrance from the high road.

I subsequently secured fifteen more of the same species, all in the same spot.

They are very local in Nice.

The females, which preponderated, were very large and brilliant, and generally far lighter in colour than those I have usually seen, especially in the mountains. They were, however, very variable in size. One specimen, a male, which I have before me, measures only 1" 1"'. Its right h.-w. is imperfectly developed, a not unusual occurrence, where there is a large number of one particular insect. Another individual and a female, from the same place, measures exactly an inch-and-a-half !

At this period they were abundant, settling on the flowers of *Onobrychis*, &c.

As a rule, the females, especially, swarmed on the flowers of *Origanum vulgare* (Wild Marjoram), to all appearance laying eggs.

Origanum is closely related to Thyme, on the latter plant of which, as has before been stated, the larva of *Arion* feeds. I may here mention that this form of the female might well be considered as a constant variety, or at least an aberration. The chief points of difference are : —

That it is larger and lighter than the typical form of the species. The dark marginal border on the f. and h.-w., are deeper black, while the crescent of spots on the f.-w. are greatly enlarged, and jet black. *The largest of these spots is exactly equal in size, to a third part of the f.-w.*

The differences from the typical form of the species, are as marked as those entitling *L. Baton v. Panoptes* or *L. Icarus v. Icarinus*, to varietal rank.

L. Arcas.

TIMES OF APPEARANCE. — July and August.

HABITAT. — ? It is to be taken in the South of France, &c.; but I have not seen an account of its capture in local works on the butterflies.

LARVA. — Unknown.

Family 4. — ERYCINIDÆ

Genus 1. — NEMEOBIUS

N. Lucina.

Times of Appearance. — May and June, and again in August. The second brood is scarcer than the former.

Habitat. — Following Millière, "On all our wooded mountains from 600 mètres (1968 feet) to 800 mètres (2624 feet) altitude." A ♀, very worn, on the Chemin de Venanson, at Saint-Martin-Vésubie, near water, June 5th 1892.

Probably at Levens, Grasse, &c.

Ovum. — Spheroid, depressed at the south pole or base, and produced at the north pole or apex ; their colour is pale glaucous. Found either singly, or in clusters of four or five on the under-side of the leaves, at the end of May and the beginning of June.

Larva. — On *Primula veris* (Primrose), *P. elatior* (Ox-lip), and various species of *Rumex*, &c.

Imago of the ♂ with only four legs fitted for walking ; the ♀ with six legs.

Family 5. — LIBYTHEIDÆ

Genus 1. — LIBYTHEA

L. Celtis.

TIMES OF APPEARANCE. — January, and again from March, to the end of July.

HABITAT. — A specimen was taken at Carabacel, (Nice), near the railway crossing, on April 16th 1889.

It is found more generally, at Cannes, Antibes, &c., at the latter of which places there are an abundance of *Celtis* trees.

LARVA. — On *Celtis australis*, (Nettle Tree), in April, May and July.

When young, it is brown with white dorsal and sub-dorsal lines.

When full-grown, it is green, with a dark dorsal stripe, the spiracles black, the lateral stripe purplish.

The entomologist Millière once found a brood of sixty larvae !

OBSERVATION. — The anterior legs rudimentary in the ♂ ; perfect in the ♀.

These characteristics have induced some writers to associate this species with the last ; in spite of its different larva, mode of pupation, &c.

The larva has been found, two thirds grown, at Cannes on May 15th.

Family 6. — APATURIDÆ

Genus 1. — CHARAXES

C. Jasius.

TIMES OF APPEARANCE. — May and June, and August and September.

HABITAT. — Nice, at Saint-Barthélemy and valley of the Mantega ; also Cannes, Antibes, &c.

LARVA.— On *Arbutus unedo* (Strawberry Tree), from May to August. The autumn larvae hybernate. Herr Seyfarth, an horticulturist of Nice, informs me that when very young this larva will feed on rose ; but that it ceases to thrive on this pabulum after a certain age.

This is not improbable ; since many small caterpillars will feed on certain succulent plants which, in a later stage of their development, they would reject.

OBSERVATION. — A specimen of *Jasius*, very worn, was taken in the back-yard of a private house at Saint-Barthélemy, (Nice), October 31st 1888, it was caught by a cock ! *Jasius* has repeatedly been seen in the neighbourhood, at different times.

It has a habit of settling on the figs as they lie drying, exposed to the sun ; but it can also be attracted by decaying animal matter, &c., thus resembling in its tastes, *A. Iris.*

Some years ago, it was abundant at the " Château ", (Nice), settling everywhere on the paths and drives ; but it is never very common, and is somewhat difficult to capture. Of course the best specimens are secured *ex larva*, *i.-e.* by rearing from the caterpillars. The French call it the " Pacha à Quatre Queues ". It is also known as the " Bashi-Bazouk."

Genus 2. — APATURA

A. Iris,

TIMES OF APPEARANCE — June and July.

HABITAT. — Neighbourhood of oak woods.

OVUM. — " Somewhat resembles a fossil *Echinus* which has lost its spines."— *Newman*.

LARVA. — On *Populus alba* (White Poplar), and *P. tremula* (Aspen Poplar), in May and June.

It is usually full-fed by the middle of June, at the latest.

VARIETY. — ab. **Jole.**

In this variety, the central band of white spots on the f.-w., and the white fascia of the h.-w. are obsolete. It is of great rarity.

OBSERVATION. — The imago of *Iris* is remarkable for its habit of frequenting oak woods, where it keeps itself at a great distance from the ground.

It may be captured by being attracted by decaying animal matter, sugar, and in dry weather, by moisture.

Another plan is to irritate the " Purple Emperor ", by throwing up pieces of paper, or tin, into the air, when the insect, enraged, descends to encounter the foe.

A. Illa ab. **Clytie.**

TIMES OF APPEARANCE.— June, and the end of August. It is double-brooded in the district.

Habitat. — Saint-Martin-Vésubie ; Venanson ; La Bollène.

A specimen of the ♂ was taken at Saint-Martin, July 15th 1889, near the torrent which flows by the village.

It had settled on the wall of the bridge, near moisture. It appears rather uncommon

Another form of the type *Ilia*, is the

Variety. — v. **Metis**.

One of the characteristics of which, is the absence of the ocellated spot on the h.-w.

Time of Appearance. — Found in May, according to Millière, in " moist places planted with willows and poplars."

Habitat. — Probably occurs at Saint-Martin, and at the Var.

Larva.— On *Salix* (Willow), and *Populus* (Poplar), in June and July.

Familly 7. — NYMPHALIDÆ

Genus 1. — LIMENITIS

L. Camilla.
TIMES OF APPEARANCE. — June to August.
HABITAT. — In Nice : in the Vallon Obscur, where it is but fairly common ; and La Trayas, near Cannes, where it is not rare ; scarce at Saint-Martin-Vésubie.

I took a very fresh specimen of *Camilla* in the " Vallon ", on June 4th 1889, also a ♂ and ♀ together, in the same spot, June 23rd 1890, and on July 29th of the same year four more, besides another seen.

LARVA. — On *Lonicera* (Honeysuckle). It passes the winter, and is full-fed in April and May.

Genus 3. — VANESSA

V. Egea.
TIMES OF APPEARANCE.— March to June, and again in September. Millière states it to be triple-brooded.

HABITAT. — Vallon Obscur, Nice ; and at Saint-Martin-Vésubie, Venanson, Cannes and many other places.

LARVA. — On *Parietaria officinalis*, in July.
VARIETY. — ab. **J.-album**.
A dark form of the summer brood.
HABITAT. — Same localities as the type.
Specimens intermediate between type and variety are not uncommon.

V. C.-album.

TIMES OF APPEARANCE. — From April to September.

HABITAT. — Generally distributed.

OVUM. — The ova are laid in May, by hybernated females. I think I saw a ♀ of either this species or else *Vanessa Egea*, deposit an egg on *Robinia Pseudo-Acacia* (Acacia), at Saint-Martin-Vésubie, July 24th 1891. The ovum was pear-shaped, if I remember, and ribbed longitudinally with grooves ; it was shiny. Its colour was dark green. The circumstance is curious, as all the known food-plants of the above-mentioned species, are in no manner related botanically to the tree on which the egg was found.

LARVA. — On Elm, Currant, Sloe, Hop, Nettle, Willow and Poplar, from May to August.

OBSERVATION. — The spring brood of *C. album* is lighter in colour than the summer form of the species.

V. Polychloros.

TIMES OF APPEARANCE. — From March to May, and from July to September.

HABITAT. — Fairly common everywhere.

OVUM. — The egg of the present species has eight longitudinal ridges, which can vary in number from seven to nine, commencing near the crown, and terminating at the base, just where the egg adheres to the twig.

LARVA. — On Elm, Sallow, Cherry, and also on *Pyrus aria* (White Beam Tree).

VARIETIES. — v. **Testudo**
and v. **Pyromelas.**

In the first-named variety the spots on the f.-w. are confluent.

Pyromelas is simply a small form of the species.

HABITAT. — Both forms are met with in the same localities as the type.

OBSERVATION.— Sometimes in bright weather hybernated specimens may be seen on the wing.

V. Urticæ.

TIMES OF APPEARANCE.— From January to December.

HABITAT. — Common everywhere.

OVUM. — " Oblong, and depressed at both extremities; at the upper extremity is a circular operculum, which is pushed off, and disappears at the time of hatching; there are generally eight longitudinal keels or ridges, extending from the operculum to the base, but this number is not constant, varying to seven and nine."— *Newman*.

In colour they are green, resembling the leaves of their food-plant. These eggs are laid in batches of sixty or eighty and sometimes a much larger number, by hybernated females, in May and June.

LARVA.— Gregarious under a web, on *Urtica dioica* (Common Nettle), and, on the authority of *The Entomologist*., January 1892, on *Humulus lupulus* (Hop), in June and July.

OBSERVATION. — Occasionally aberrations of *Urticae* occur, in which the dorsal and median spots on the f.-w. are in abeyance, somewhat resembling the variety *Ichnusa*; but these varieties have not the same outline as *Ichnusa*, which is confined to Corsica and Sardinia.

V. Io.

TIMES OF APPEARANCE. — April to October, the imagines hybernating.

HABITAT. — Common on the coast; but very scarce in the mountains.

OVUM. — Eggs in April and May.

LARVA. — On *Urtica dioica* and *Humulus lupulus* (Hop), from June to August.

VARIETY. — ab. **Joides**.

It is merely a small form of the species, and is not confined to any particular locality.

V. Antiopa.

TIMES OF APPEARANCE. — From March to May, and from June to October.

HABITAT. — Nice, in the Vallon Obscur; Cannes; Saint-Martin-Vésubie, near the torrent; and many other places. Very common.

OVUM. — Laid in the spring by hybernated females.

LARVA. — Lives in company on *Salix alba*, and sometimes on Birch, Poplar and Nettle, from June to August.

VARIETY. — ab. **Hygiaea**.

The white, or light yellow hind marginal band is much broader than in the typical form, and the blue spots are either entirely, or partially absent.

HABITAT. — The same localities as the type. It is very rare.

OBSERVATION. — The individuals of the March brood are hybernated specimens.

V. Atalanta.

TIMES OF APPEARANCE. — June to October, and after hybernation, in the spring.

It has been seen on the wing in Nice, as early as January 10th.

HABITAT. — Common everywhere.

OVUM. — The eggs are laid singly.

LARVA. — Solitary under a web, on Nettle and *Parietaria officinalis*, from June to September. On the coast it is found in the spring, and has been collected as early as April 1st, full-fed.

V. Cardui.

TIMES OF APPEARANCE. — March to June after hybernation, and from July to September.

Millière states that it flies " even in December and January."

HABITAT. — Very common everywhere, occurring up to a height of 8000 feet and over, in the mountains.

OVUM. — Laid singly, low down on the plant, generally towards the end of June.

LARVA. — On various species of *Carduus*, on *Echium vulgare* (Viper's Bugloss), and accidentally on *Parietaria*, from June to August.

Genus 4. — MELITÆA

M. Cynthia.

TIMES OF APPEARANCE. — July and August.

HABITAT. — Saint-Martin-Vésubie, on the Balme de la Frema, and at the Madone des Fenêtres, near the lake.

I have taken it on four consecutive seasons, (1889-92), either as larvae or imagines.

On July 24th 1889, several specimens were taken; and also on July 14th and 23rd 1890, Most of those seen on the latter occasion, however, were *passé*.

Larva. — On *Plantago lanceolata* and several other species of Plantain, in June.

Many larvae, full-fed, as well as pupae were found on the Balme, June 25th 1889. On June 28th 1891, I found four caterpillars, and several chrysalids. The first imago of these latter, emerged on July 9th of the same summer.

Pupa. — Suspended, on grass and other low-growing herbage.

M. Aurinia v. Provincialis, Boisd.
and v. Iberica, Oberth.
Desfontaines, H. S.

Times of Appearance. — May to August.

Habitat. — (of *v. Iberica*), Mt. Vinaigrier, Nice ; and Saint-Martin-Vésubie, on the Chemin de Venanson. I have never taken the *var. Provincialis*, and, in fact, am in doubt of its existence in the Maritime Alps.

Iberica has been taken, in very worn condition at Saint-Martin, on July 4th to 6th 1890; and on June 23rd 1891 I captured a ♂ specimen, fresh. I cannot be sure whether the insects caught in the mountains are *Provincialis* or *Iberica* ; but in the case of those taken in Nice, I have it on the authority of D[r] Staudinger, that they are of the latter variety.

Ovum. — (of *Aurinia* type), Somewhat flattened on the crown. The eggs of this species are laid on the under-side of those leaves nearest the ground, from the beginning to the middle of June.

Larva. — (of *Aurinia*), On *Scabiosa succisa*, *Teucrium Scorodina*, *Digitalis purpurea*, *Centranthus ruber* and Plantain, from March to September.

I have always found these larvae (*Iberica*), on *Centranthus ruber* (Red Valerian), though it is not usually stated in books as feeding on this plant.

On April 18th and May 14th 1889, I found a great many larvae; and on the latter date, pupae on Mt. Vinaigrier.

Pupa. — The chrysalids fastened in the crevices of walls, &c.

Observation. — At Saint-Martin, the species seems to frequent the neighbourhood of hazel bushes which cover the hill side, where it is common. This variety, as its name implies, is usually supposed to be confined to Spain and Portugal.

It must not be confounded with *M. Desfontanii* of Godt, a totally distinct species.

M. Cinxia.

Times of Appearance. — April, May, June and August.

Habitat. — Common.

Ovum. — Laid in batches on the food-plant, in May and June.

Larva. — On *Plantago lanceolata*, *Hieracium pilosella* and *Veronica*, from April to May, and from August to September.

It is stated by Millière, that this larva when young lives in society, and passes the winter under a common web; in this stage it is only in its third moult.

M. Phœbe.

Times of Appearance. — May to August.

Habitat. — Saint-Martin-Vésubie, Berthemont and other localities. Not uncommon.

Larva. — On *Centaurea jacea*, from May to September.

M. Didyma.

Times of Appearance. — May to August.

Habitat. — Cannes, Nice, Saint-Martin-Vésubie, Berthemont, and other spots. Generally distributed.

Larva. — On *Plantago*, &c., from April to June.

Varieties. — The present species, like all of the genus is very variable.

The females, which are darker than the males, range in colour from a light brown to deep black, varied by a few spots of a lighter shade. This very dark form most resembles the variety *Meridionalis*, which, however, does not occur in the department.

The other variety, which does not appear to be mentioned in the local faunas, is the

v. Occidentalis.

Habitat. — In South Europe it is found in the same localities as the type.

Observation. — *Didyma* is, without doubt, the most subject to variation of all the species composing the genus. Staudinger, in his *Lepidopteren-Liste*, enumerates no less than eleven well-marked varieties.

Specimens are found, from time to time, in which the ground colour of the wings is entirely white. This condition is owing to the absence of pigment in the scales.

M. Dejone ?

Time of Appearance. — June.

Habitat. — In the European works, it is stated as being found in " the South of France ", &c. Its occurrence in the district is, perhaps, rather improbable.

I have seen no accounts of its capture.

LARVA. — Undescribed.

M. Athalia.

TIMES OF APPEARANCE. — May to August.

HABITAT. — Common everywhere.

LARVA. — On *Plantago* and *Melampyrum sylvaticum*, from May to September.

VARIETIES. — The varieties of this species, perhaps, above all other *Melitaeae*, are the most remarkable.

Individuals occasionally occur, in which several of the central rows of deep fulvous or black spots on the f.-w., are confluent.

This deviation from the common form, gives the insect the appearance of having a thick black band in the middle of the wings.

Another variety, which most approaches the variety *Navarina*, has the f.-w. almost entirely suffused with dark fulvous.

There are various other aberrations from the typical form, which, however, it would be unprofitable to enumerate.

ab. **Corythalia**, the f.-w. are more broadly fulvous than in the type.

ab. **Navarina** has the wings almost entirely black above, with hind marginal fulvous band.

M. Parthenie.

TIMES OF APPEARANCE. — June and August.

HABITAT. — Saint-Martin-Vésubie, at the Col de Saint-Martin; also on the Balme, and is also found at the Madone, Berthemont and Thorenc. A sub-alpine species.

Larva. — On *Plantago*, in April.

Variety. — v. **Varia.**

This is the true Alpine variety of the species, and is found at a higher elevation than the type. It is smaller than *Parthenie* and the female is darker, and clouded with greenish black. Both sexes have the central row of spots on the u.-s. of the h.-w. white, instead of yellow.

I have found both type and variety, also a *formâ intermedia*, or intermediate form of the two species. It is common at these high elevations.

Genus 5. — ARGYNNIS

A. **Euphrosyne.**

Times of Appearance. — May and June, and again in August.

Habitat. — Vence-Cagnes ; and at Saint-Martin, where it is found at the Cascade and the Madone. On June 19th 1891, I captured a ♂ of *Euphrosyne*, fresh, at the Cascade.

Ovum. — According to M[r] Buckler, quoted by Newman in his *British Butterflies*, it is " of a blunt, conical shape, with its lower surface which adheres to the leaf, flattened ; its sides are ribbed : at first it is of a dull greenish-yellow colour, becoming afterwards brownish." It occurs in May and June.

Larva. — On *Viola canina*, in June and September.

A. **Pales.**

Times of Appearance. — July and August.

Habitat. — Mt. Balme de la Frema, at the summit ; and at the Madone, to the east of Saint-Martin-Vésubie.

It is only found on the higher Alpine Passes. Fairly common.

Larva. — On *Viola montana*, *V. canina* and other species of violets, in July.

Variety. — ab. **Napaea.**
The ♂ is tinged with sulphur yellow beneath; ♀ greenish above.

Habitat. — Same as the type

Observation. — It varies ; specimens intermediate between type and variety being met with, as in the case of *M. Parthenie* and the *var. Varia*, &c.

In some instances, insects of specific rank possessing no varieties, bear some of the characters of another, and totally distinct butterfly.

A. Dia.
Times of Appearance. — May to September.

Habitat. — Vence-Cagnes, near the river ; and at Cannes. Not uncommon.

I took a specimen, fresh, at Cagnes, on April 9th 1889.

Larva. — On *Viola canina*, *V. tricolor* and other kinds of Violets, in July and September.

A. Amathusia.
Time of Appearance. — July.

Habitat. — At Saint-Martin-Vésubie, it is found on Mt. Colmiane, the summit of the Balme de la Frema, and at the Madone des Fenêtres.

An alpine butterfly, and somewhat local, though common where it occurs.

On July 14th 1890, I captured five males and two females in a little field at the side of the road, about half a mil before reaching the Madone itself.

They were common, though most of them were rather worn, at this date.

It is a curious circumstance, that nearly all the specimens taken had either one of the f.-w. or else one of the h.-w. much smaller than its fellow, and it was generally in a crumpled state. I have noticed the same thing in the ease of *A. Belia, E. Cassiope* and *S. Lavaterae*, but not to this extent.

On July 22nd, I took a very fresh ♂ specimen on the Balme. At this great altitude plants and insects are somewhat later in appearance, than at a lower elevation.

They are consequently to be met with till a later date.

LARVA. — On *Polygonum bistorta*, in May.

A. Daphne.

TIMES OF APPEARANCE. — May to August.

HABITAT. — It is found on the high-road to Nice, about a mile before the village of Saint-Martin-Vésubie; on the ascent to the Balme de la Frema; and on the road leading from Saint-Martin to Venanson.

I took a ♀ on the Chemin de Venanson.

It is never very common, but it is most frequent flying round bramble bushes in the full sun, on the Route de Nice.

LARVA. — On *Rubus idaeus* (Raspberry), in May.

A. Hecate.

TIMES OF APPEARANCE. — June and July.

HABITAT. — It is a mountain species. Millière says it is rare.

LARVA. — Unknown.

A. Lathonia.

TIMES OF APPEARANCE. — May to September.
HABITAT. — Saint-Martin-Vésubie ; Berthemont ; Levens, &c., where it is commonly distributed.
OVUM. — Solitary, in August or September.
LARVA. — Feeds solitarily on *Viola tricolor* and *Onobrychis*, in May and August.
VARIETY. — ab. **Valdensis**.
An aberrant form, in which the silver spots are confluent.

A. Aglaja.

TIMES OF APPEARANCE. — May to September.
HABITAT. — Saint-Martin-Vésubie, on the Chemin de Venanson ; Mt. Colmiane ; Mt. Balme de la Frema, and many other places. Common.
OVUM. — Eggs in August.
LARVA. — On *Viola canina* and *Polygonum bistorta*, in May and June.

P. *bistorta* is not mentioned in the books as a food-plant of the species, though larvae were found in abundance on this plant, on the Colmiane, on July 1st 1889.

The butterflies emerged three weeks afterwards. I do not possess any imagines from caterpillars found on this occasion, but have seen several of them, which appear smaller in size than those from a lower elevation.

VARIETY. — ab. **Charlotta**, ♀.
In this form, " the silver spots on the u.-s. are larger than in the type, there being especially three large basal silvery blotches ; occasionally the spots of the central row coalesce to form bands." *(Lg.)*

A. Niobe.

Times of Appearance. — July and August.

Habitat. — According to Millière, "it flies in mountainous regions."

Larva. — On *Viola tricolor* and *odorata*, in May.

Varieties. — ab. **Eris**
and ab. **Pelopia.**

The u.-s. of the h.-w. have the light spots changed to pale yellow, without any trace of silver. Occasionally a faint silvery tinge is seen in the light markings, as in *Niobe*. Specimens, in fact, are met with intermediate between type and variety.

Habitat. — At Saint-Martin-Vésubie and mountainous districts generally; — it is found on the Route de Venanson; Mt. Colmiane; and the Balme de la Frema.

This variety is the form of the insect most usually met with.

ab. *Pelopia*, Bork, has the wings suffused with black by the extension of the dark markings.

It may here be well to mention that individuals of this genus are sometimes to be seen, whose wings bear white patches or traces of markings of a light colour. The reason for this condition has already been stated. The same thing may be observed in the case of *Erebia Cassiope* and *Epinephile Janira*. It is known by dealers as *albedine infecta*.

A. Adippe.

Times of Appearance. — May to July.

Habitat. — Fairly common everywhere.

It is also found in the mountains, but not at any great height.

Ovum. — In August.

Larva. — On *Viola odorata* and *tricolor*, in May and June.

Variety. — ab. Cleodoxa.

Corresponds to the variety *Eris* of *A. Niobe*.

Habitat. — Same as the type. It is to be found at Saint-Martin-Vésubie, though it is not abundant.

A. Paphia.

Times of Appearance. — July and August.

Habitat. — It is common on the coast and in the mountain districts, as at La Bollène, Saint-Martin, &c.

Ovum. — It is whitish, and is laid singly.

Mr Newman, in his very interesting book, relates that the eggs of *Paphia* are laid on dead leaves or moss, or on the living leaves of *Viola canina* and *odorata*, at the end of July and beginning of August.

Larva. — On *Viola canina* and *V. odorata*, from the end of May to the middle of June.

Varieties. — ab. Valesina, ♀
and v. Anargyra.

The former is a dimorphic condition of the female, in which the wings are dark blackish brown, with black spots.

Habitat. — Same as the type.

It is to be met with in the fields near the torrent, at Saint-Martin-Vésubie; and also near the Col de Saint-Martin, on the ascent of the Balme de la Frema.

v. *Anargyra* has the silver streaks absent from the u.-s. of the h.-w. Rare.

A. Pandora.

TIMES OF APPEARANCE. — June and July.

HABITAT.— Roquebillière, La Bollène, Saint-Martin-Vésubie, and other places. It is rare.

LARVA. — On *Viola tricolor*, in May.

Family 8. — SATYRIDÆ

Genus 1. — MELANARGIA

M. Galathea v. Procida.

TIMES OF APPEARANCE. — June to August.

HABITAT. — Generally distributed. It also occurs in the mountains, though it does not extend to any great elevation.

OVUM. — " The eggs are laid at random, the parent female not selecting any particular species of plant. The eggs thus deposited, find their way by the simple power of gravitation to the roots of the grass, there to take their chance of hatching and future well-doing. The egg, which is perfectly hard and dry, and free from any glutinous covering, is white and almost spherical, but is slightly flattened at both its poles " .... — From Newman's " *British Butterflies* ".

LARVA.— (of typical *Galathea*), On *Phleum pratense* and other grasses, in April and May. The ♂ larva is usually brown ; and the ♀, green.

OBSERVATION.—The type is not found in the Maritime Alps. Other varieties are

ab. **Leucomelas** ♀, and

ab. **Galene**.

In *Leucomelas*, a variety confined to the female, the markings are entirely absent from the u.-s. of the h.-w. which are quite white, the black markings on the upper surface only, showing through.

ab. *Galene* has the ocellated spots absent.

M. Syllius
Psyche, Hub.

Times of Appearance. — May and the beginning of June.

Habitat. — Route de Villefranche near Nice, on rocky ground near the sea; Villefranche; Saint-Jean; gorge of Saint-André, near Nice; Iles des Lérins off Cannes.

It is local; but abundant where it occurs.

Larva. — On *Brachypodium pinnatum*, in May.

The following, which I quote with certain omissions from Lang. But. Eur. vol. I, p. 236, is translated from Millière; " At this time (May 10th to 15th, *i. e.*, when it is full-grown), it is rather elongated, pubescent, of a yellowish flesh-colour, with well-marked and continuous lines.

The vascular line is large, of a clear brown, and bordered narrowly with white on each side. The subdorsal line is Naples-yellow, and is edged with green above and below; stigmatal line fine and clear. The head is globular, pubescent, and of an indistinct green, with two black ocelli on each side.

The legs are flesh coloured........

The stigmata are very small, white, encircled with black.

Caterpillars can vary from the normal colour, to bright green with a black vascular line.

Pupa. — According to the same authority, it is " Rather elongated, plump, and smooth, yellowish in colour, and finely striped with dark brown."

Variety. — ab. **Ixora**.

The ocelli are wanting from the u.-s. of the h.-w.

Genus 2. — EREBIA

E. Epiphron v. Cassiope.

TIMES OF APPEARANCE. — June and July.

HABITAT.— At Saint-Martin-Vésubie :— Mt. Siruol ; Balme de la Frema ; Madone des Fenêtres ; Col de Saint-Dalmas, and many other places. It is common at these heights.

LARVA. — (of *Cassiope*), On *Poa annua* and *Festuca ovina*.

OBSERVATION. — The type *Epiphron*, contrary to Millière, does not belong to the entomological fauna of the department.

It is, perhaps, here well to observe, that all known pupae of this alpine genus, are not attached by the tail, but placed in an upright position among grass, near the ground.

E. Cassiope, as has already been pointed out, is subject to albinism ; specimens being occasionally caught, whose wings bear marks or traces of marks of a light colour.

The spots on both the f. and h.-w. can also be partially or entirely absent.

E. Melampus.

TIMES OF APPEARANCE. — July and August.

HABITAT. — Mt. Balme de la Frema, &c., at Saint-Martin-Vésubie ; and, following Millière, also at Berthemont.

It is much less common than the former.

On August 2nd 1890, I captured a good specimen at the Madone ; and on August 11th, I caught two more on the Balme (or Baume) de la Frema. They were all forwarded to Dr Staudinger, who certified them to be *Melampus*. I have also usually done this in the case of most species of whose identity I have been doubtful.

LARVA. — Unknown.

E. Mnestra.

TIMES OF APPEARANCE. — July and August.

HABITAT. — Balme (or Baous) de la Frema, at Saint-Martin-Vésubie. Rare.

On August 11th, I captured a ♀ in the above-mentioned locality.

LARVA. — Unknown.

VARIETY. — v. Gorgophone, *Bell*.
Larger than the type.

E. Pharte.

TIMES OF APPEARANCE. — July and August.

HABITAT. — I know of no particular locality.

It ought, according to the works on lepidoptera, to be found in the same places as the others of the genus already enumerated. Millière does not appear to have met with it, or *Mnestra*.

LARVA. — Unknown.

E. Manto.

TIMES OF APPEARANCE. — July and August.

HABITAT. — " Prairies élevées de la haute Vésubie 2000 mètres (6560 feet) environ."— *Mil*.

LARVA. — Unknown.

VARIETIES. — ab. Bubastis
and   v. Pyrrhula (?).

The former variety differs from the type in the h.-w. having a white band ; ♀ with differently marked cilia or fringes.

E. Ceto.

TIMES OF APPEARANCE. — July and August.

HABITAT.— Saint-Martin-Vésubie, near the village ; Balme de la Frema ; Madone ; Cascade ; and at Berthemont-les-Bains. Common.

I took it on one occasion, in a little field off the mule path, about half-a-mile from the Madone des Fenêtres, on July 14th 1890, when five males and eight females were captured in the course of a few minutes. The spot literally swarmed with them ; in fact, it was about the only species of *Erebia* represented.

LARVA. — Unknown.

VARIETY. — v. Phorcys.

The submarginal spots on the u.-s. are white, with dark brown centres.

OBSERVATION. — At the time of the capture of *Ceto*, a specimen of what was apparently the variety *Phorcys* was taken. Dr Staudinger does not appear to acknowledge this form.

E. Medusa.

TIMES OF APPEARANCE. — May and June.

HABITAT. — According to the late A. Risso, " High mountains of the Maritime Alps."

LARVA.— On *Panicum sanguinale* and other Grasses, in April and May.

E. Stygne.

TIME OF APPEARANCE. — July.

HABITAT.— Saint-Martin-Vésubie, on all the neighbouring mountains, such as the Conchet, &c.
LARVA. — Unknown.
VARIETY. — v. Pyrenaica.
This form appears to be here more widely distributed than the type.
HABITAT. — Found in the same localities as *Stygne*.

E. Evias.
TIMES OF APPEARANCE. — July.
HABITAT. — Saint-Martin-Vésubie, on the Chemin de Venanson, where it is common ; Mt. Balme de la Frema; Cascade (Borréon); Madone des Fenêtres, &c.
The ♀, which has a light grey band on the u.-s. of the h.-w., like the ♀ of *E. Mnestra*, is rare.
I caught a specimen of this sex on the Route de Venanson, July 9th 1891.

E. Epistygne.
TIMES OF APPEARANCE. — March and July.
HABITAT. — " Heights of Grasse."— *Mil*.
LARVA. — Unknown.

E. Tyndarus.
TIMES OF APPEARANCE. — June to the middle of August.
HABITAT. — Mts. Tournairet, Siruol, Balme de la Frema, near Saint-Martin-Vésubie ; and Madone des Fenêtres. It occurs only at a great elevation, higher than any of the preceding.
I have seen it on the Pepiori, a higher spur of the Balme, at an altitude of 9000 feet above the sea level. It is common at these heights. A fresh specimen,

among other worn ones, was taken on August 31st one season. The wings of this species, as is the case with *E. Cassiope*, &c., can be entirely without the small black spots. Distinguished from the next, among other things, by the slight violet sheen of the wings.

LARVA. — Unknown.

VARIETIES. — v. Cæcodromus and v. Dromus.

The former of these two varieties differs from the type in the absence of the fulvous bands and ocelli.

Dromus has the fulvous bands broader and redder than in the typical form, and the ocellated spots are larger.

HABITATS. — Found in the same spots as the type.

OBSERVATION. — Specimens intermediate between the type and *Dromus* are frequent. At Saint-Martin, the typical insect is somewhat uncommon, and the *var. Dromus*, though not very abundant is scarcer than this *forma intermedia*.

The ♀ is lighter in colour than the ♂; and the u.-s. of the f.-w. is pale fulvous inclining to yellowish; the marbled grey, too, of the h.-w. is also tinged with yellow.

E. Gorge.

TIMES OF APPEARANCE. — July and August.

HABITAT. — At or near Saint-Martin-Vésubie, it has been taken on June 26th (1891) at the Madone, and a ♀, very large, on the Balme, July 4th (1890). It is not very common.

LARVA. — Unknown.

VARIETY. — ab. **Erynis**.

The ocelli are absent from all the wings. Here, the *var. Erynis*, or rather a form intermediate between type and variety seem to be of more frequent occurrence.

OBSERVATION. — I am rather disposed to believe that the *v. Gorgone, Boisd*, is to be found in the department, but refrain from admitting it to a place in the rhopalocera of the district, till its position has been really established. It occurs in the Pyrenees.

E. Goante.

TIMES OF APPEARANCE. — July and August.

HABITAT. — In the neighbourhood of Saint-Martin (formerly known as Saint-Martin-Lantosque) it is found at the Madone, and in the Borréon, near the Cascade.

I captured a large specimen of the ♂ in the former place, on the mountain side facing the hotel, August 2nd 1890, after a hot chase. Another ♂, of considerably over the average size, was taken in or near the grounds of the little inn at the Cascade, August 10th 1891.

At these dates, the specimens were very fresh. It appears to be somewhat scarce.

LARVA. — Unknown.

VARIETY. — v. **Gorgone** ♀, *H. S.* (?)

It is smaller than the type, and is stated as belonging to the Pyrenees, though it is not unlikely as the type exists in the department, that this variety of the female may occur here also.

E. Neoridas.

Times of Appearance. — End of June to August.

Habitat. — Saint-Martin-Vésubie, where it is abundant everywhere; also at the Cascade, in the Borréon valley; and on the ascent to the Balme de la Frema up to a height of from 7000 to 7500 feet.

Larva. — I have partially succeeded in rearing the larva, which up to the present has remained undiscovered, from the egg. The results of my investigations may perhaps prove interesting to entomologists.

The process was carried out in the manner already described, with very young larvae.

On September 22nd of last year, I induced an impregnated female to lay. At this date it commenced by depositing one egg, subsequently laying six or eight daily, till the number reached twenty. Three days later, the ova changed from their normal white colour to pale pink.

On the 27th inst. these same turned to a grey colour, the sculptured grooves changing to black.

Sixteen days from this, on October 12th; the first caterpillar emerged, and larvae continued to come out up to the 19th of the same month.

The last one perished to my great regret, on December 15th.

They were fed on the tenderest shoots of *Poa annua*, as it is on this plant that the caterpillar of *E. Aethiops*, to which it bears the closest affinity, lives.

They were also fed on *Panicum sanguinale* with but small success.

These larvae come forth from the top of the egg,

nibbling a circular piece out of the shell in such a way as to leave a kind of lid appended.

The first thing they do after birth, is to set to at once devouring their quondam cradle.

Their appearance when first hatched is brownish.

The following is a correct description, when twelve days old.

Length 2‴. Pale green with darker dorsal stripe, and white lateral line ; head lighter.

Three days previous to this they had retained their brown colour. The early stages of the *Erebiae*, which are very little known are worthy of a closer attention than they have hitherto received.

OBSERVATION. — *Neoridas* is variable in size and markings, some species appearing so different from the usual form, as to sometimes lead even experienced lepidopterists to believe they have met with a totally distinct species. I take occasion to mention this here, as the same thing is observeable in the case of many butterflies, but some insects more than others, and will save my alluding to it, in the future. These aberrant forms would well repay study, in view of a correct discrimination between accepted forms and occasional varieties.

E. Aethiops.

TIMES OF APPEARANCE. — July to September.

HABITAT. — " Thorenc and Taulanne valleys, where it is common." — *Mil.*

I am not aware that it is taken at Saint-Martin itself, though it has a very extensive European distribution.

Ovum. — According to Mr Buckler, page 65 of no. 75 of the *Entomologist's Monthly Magazine.*, " The egg may be called large for the size of the fly, and is nearly globular, though somewhat ovate in shape, and placed on end ; the shell is glistening and ribbed, but not deeply, with about thirty longitudinal ribs, and with very shallow transverse reticulations, in colour pale greenish-yellow, and afterwards pale pinkish-gray, speckled with claret-brown."
The ova deposited in the autumn, hatch in about fourteen days, the larvae hybernating.

Larva. — On *Dactylis* and various species of *Poa*, in May and June, after hybernation, and again in October.

E. Newman in *British Butterflies*, vol. I, page 83, states that the caterpillar of *Aethiops* will feed, in confinement, on *Agrostis canina*.

E. Ligea.

Times of Appearance. — July and August.

Habitat. — Saint-Martin-Vésubie : on the Chemin de Venanson ; Balme de la Frema, but not at any considerable elevation ; and the Borréon.

On June 29th or 30th 1889, I took a single specimen of the ♂, very worn, which had probably been hybernating, in a little piece of land off the Route de Venanson. On July 24th of the same year, several more were captured on the ascent to the Balme, not very for from the top.

Larva. — On *Milium*, *Poa* and other Grasses, in March, April and September.

OBSERVATION.— Local; but abundant where it occurs. The ♀ is much less common than the ♂.

E. Euryale.
TIMES OF APPEARANCE. — July and August.
HABITAT. — Same as the last.
On July 24th, several specimens were taken on the Balme, among the pine trees. It does not ascend to any considerable height.
LARVA. — On Grasses, in June and July.
OBSERVATION. — Very variable. The slight traces of a grey band on the u.-s. of the h.-w. are subject to variation, being sometimes distinct and occasionally entirely wanting ; the spots too, are liable to the same condition.
The female, as in the preceding species, is much scarcer than the male.

Genus 3. — OENEIS

O. Aëllo.
TIMES OF APPEARANCE. — End of June and beginning of July.
HABITAT. — Mts. Pepiori and Balme de la Frema, near the summit ; and also at the Madone des Fenêtres, from a height of from 6000 feet upwards. Not very common.
On July 24th 1889, I captured three specimens, very worn, in the two first of these spots, and others were, I believe, taken by our party at the time. I have received information from a most reliable source, that it has been taken at the Madone, in front of the hotel doors !

I must not omit to here mention that I caught a ♂ and ♀ on the Balme, on June 27th of last year (1891).

They were very fresh, and had evidently not been long on the wing.

Ovum. — The species has been known to lay even after impalement.

Larva. — Unknown.

Probably lives on Grasses, as do all larvae of the genus that are already known.

Observation. — *Aëllo* only occurs at a considerable elevation, being found on the verge of the snow line. In Switzerland it is taken in alternate years.

Genus 4. — SATYRUS

S. Hermione.

Times of Appearance. — July and August.

Habitat. — Nice and Saint-Martin-Vésubie, where it is common.

Larva. — On *Holcus lanatus* and other Grasses, in May, after hybernation.

S. Alcyone.

Times of Appearance. — July and August.

Habitat. — Same as the last species. It is less common than *Hermione*.

Larva. — Undescribed.

S. Circe.

Times of Appearance. — From the middle of June, to the end of August, according to the altitude of its locality.

HABITAT. — Nice, in the Vallon Obscur; Saint-Martin-Vésubie, on the Chemin de Venanson ; on the Route de Nice, everywhere ; Berthemont-les-Bains, and many other places. Common.

I took a ♀, which had freshly emerged from the pupa, on June 21st 1890.

LARVA. — On *Lolium perenne*, and other Grasses. It is a night-feeder, and is obtained by searching at dusk with a lantern ; in the day time it hides under stones.

PUPA. — Not suspended ; it rests in a slight hollow in the ground.

OBSERVATION. — This species is the largest and most striking of the family ; it is also one of the largest European butterflies.

S. Briseis.

TIMES OF APPEARANCE. — July and August.

HABITAT. — Saint-Martin-Vésubie, on the Chemin de Venanson ; Saint-Dalmas ; Route de Nice ; Berthemont ; Levens, frequenting hot rocky situations.

The specimens from Saint-Dalmas are, I think, the finest I have yet seen.

In the autumn of 1888, I took several ♀. One of these, which is in my collection, measures 2" 8''', and is of a very light hue.

LARVA.— On Grasses, and according to Dr Hofmann, on Heath, in May and June, in which latter month it is full-fed.

VARIETY. — v. **Pirata**, ♀.

Differs from the type above, in the colour of the light bands, which are dull ochre-yellow, instead of white ; beneath, the h.-w. are less varied, being much lighter at the base ; the central light band is wanting, and the whole wing is greyer in colouring than in *Briseis.*

HABITAT. — Same as the type.

S. Semele.

TIMES OF APPEARANCE. — July to September.

HABITAT. — It is found all along the coast ; in the mountains, where it is common, it occurs most frequently on the Chemin de Venanson, and on the zig-zags on the ascent of the Balme de la Frema.

OVUM. — In July.

LARVA. — On *Triticum repens* and other grasses, in May after hybernation, and again in the autumn.

The caterpillar hides beneath the surface of the earth, or under stones during the day, quitting its hiding-place only at night, when it feeds. Mr Edward Newman in *British Butterflies,* says that he has reared the species on *Aira cæspitosa* and *praecox.*

OBSERVATION. — *Semele,* like *Circe* and many other butterflies, has a habit of assimilating itself with the rocks and stony ground on which it rests in repose, and which in colour and markings, it much resembles.

It is rather difficult to capture, on account of its great alertness.

Some of the ♀ *Semele* are of great size.

S. Statilinus.

TIMES OF APPEARANCE. — July and August.

HABITAT. — Saint-Martin-Vésubie : on the Chemin de Venanson ; Route de Nice, &c.; it also occurs, among other places in Nice, in the Vallon Obscur. Has the habits of the last species and is common.

Ovum. — It has been known to deposit fertile eggs of its own accord.

Larva. — Appears to be undescribed.

Girard quotes Maurice Sand, who says, " it feeds on Grasses in woods, during June, and that it is easy to procure by sweeping, at night." (p. 213).

Variety. — v. Allionia.

Larger and paler than the type ; the ♀ has the black spots distinctly ringed with yellow. U. S.: paler and more uniform than in the type, the white band indistinct or else absent ; near the hind margin are some whitish spots.

Habitat. — Same as the type ; though it is not as common.

I took a specimen of *Allionia* in the Vallon Obscur, on July 29th 1890.

S. Fidia.

Time of Appearance. — July.

Habitat. — " It frequents little wooded mountains ".,
— *Mil.*

Larva. — On *Piptaterum multiflorum* and other Grasses, in March and May. Millière says it prefers the former. (See Appendix of Plants).

Pupa. — Is not suspended ; but lies free on the ground ; it is of a brown colour.

S. Dryas.

Phaedra, Linn.

Times of Appearance. — From July to August.

Habitat.—Venanson, in the valley, on the Colmiane side ; and is very abundant on the Route de Nice, about 53 kilomètres from the latter town.

On July 21st (1891), the season being later than usual, no *Dryas* were observed on the Chemin de Nice ; but on the 30th inst., several, among others ♀ were either seen, or taken.

Larva. — On *Avena elatior*, in June.

It is found in woods.

Pupa.— " At the end of June, it becomes a rounded brown-coloured pupa, not suspended, but placed on the ground, in a kind of small earthy cocoon ".,— *Girard*.

Observation. — Very variable ; some ♀ having considerable expanse of wing ; the blue spot on the f.-w. is occasionally very large.

Frequents hot, dry situations and the vicinity of bushes in flower, and is somewhat local ; but common where it occurs. The ♀ generally emerge from the chrysalids, about a week or more after the appearance of the ♂.

S. Actaea.

Times of Appearance. — June and July.

Habitat. — Valley of the Madone, near Saint-Martin-Vésubie ; Route de Venanson ; Chemin de Nice ; La Bollène, &c.

It is especially common in the first of these places, frequenting hot, stony spots, and is rather difficult to take.

Larva. — Unknown.

VARIETY. — **Peas**, ♀.

In the v. *Peas*, ♀, all the wings above, have an ochreous band. U.-s. of h.-w. whitish, with a central band of dark grey. Millière states that the *var. Podarce* of Portugal and Syria occurs in the department.

S. Cordula.

TIMES OF APPEARANCE. — June and July.

HABITAT. — Saint-Martin-Vésubie, &c.

It is very common on the Chemin de Venanson; also in the Valley of the Madone, and on the Route de Nice, among many other places.

LARVA. — Unknown.

OBSERVATION. — *Cordula* must not be confused with the last, which in some points it greatly resembles, and of which it was formerly considered to be a variety.

I think it has perhaps, most affinity to the ♂ *Dryas*. Same habits as *Actaea*.

Genus 5. — PARARGE

P. Mæra.

TIMES OF APPEARANCE. — April to September.

HABITAT. — Commonly distributed.

OVUM. — On July 24th (1891), at Saint-Martin, I found an egg freshly deposited on a blade of grass. The caterpillar emerged on August 2nd. About October, it ceased feeding, evidently preparatory to hybernation; but on December 15th, after an abstinence of nearly three months, it began to eat again.

The ovum is round and white, and is usually laid on the upper surface of the plant.

Larva. — On *Festuca ovina, Poa annua* and other Grasses, in April and June.

Pupa. — Green or greenish black, rather angulated, with two dorsal rows of yellow or white spots. I have found it suspended to rocks in sheltered positions, on the Route de Venanson and at the Cascade. When empty, it presents a white, transparent appearance.

Variety. — v. **Adrasta**.
This is a mountain form of the insect. It is slightly larger than the type, and is very dark brown. On the wing it has much the same appearance as an *Erebia*, with which I have sometimes confounded it ; so dark is its general aspect and colouring.

Habitat. — Borréon, where it is common ; but is rather less abundant at Saint-Martin itself.

On June 13th 1891, I captured four ♂ and one ♀, in the former locality.

P. Megœra.

Times of Appearance. — Throughout the year, in fine weather.

Habitat. — Common everywhere. It has much the same habits as the last.

Ovum. — At the end of May.

Larva. — On Grasses from March to April, and from June to July. Millière gives September, as well.

Pupa. — Which is green, is suspended to walls. I found what was apparently a chrysalis of this species, near Gairaut to the north of Nice, suspended to an aperture of a wall, May 3rd 1891. It had only just changed to the pupal state.

VARIETY. — Specimens are met with, which are intermediate between the type and the *v. Lyssa*. This latter, I may add, is only found in Dalmatia, and one or two other spots in the East of Europe.

P. Aegeria.

TIMES OF APPEARANCE. — April to August.

HABITAT. — It is met with everywhere; and is supposed to have a predilection for walls, whence it is called the " Wall Butterfly."

OVUM. — The eggs " are almost spherical in figure, the entire surface being reticulated with minute ridges, which divide into hexagonal cells, and give it the appearance of being honeycombed." — *Newman*. The larvae, when first hatched are a dingy brown colour.

LARVA. — On grasses, especially *Triticum repens*, in March, May, June, September and October.

PUPA. — Green, with a double row of dorsal tubercles; on walls, &c.

VARIETY. — v. **Egerides**.

Is darker than the typical *Egeria*, and a southern form of the insect. It is found in the same localities as the type.

TIMES OF APPEARANCE. — April, July and August.

Genus 6. — EPINEPHILE

E. Lycaon.

TIMES OF APPEARANCE. — From May to July.

HABITAT. — Saint-Martin-Vésubie, on the Route de Venanson; Mt. Colmiane. Common.

LARVA. — On Grasses, in May and July.

On July 9th of last year (1891), I found a caterpillar, full-fed, under some stones on the Colmiane.

It began to pupate next day, and the imago, a ♀, emerged soon after, on July 30th.

PUPA. — Is green or brown varied with pink streaks. The chrysalis from which my *Lycaon* came forth, was of the former variety.

E. Janira.

TIMES OF APPEARANCE. — June to September.

HABITAT. — Generally distributed on the coast, and in the mountains.

OVUM. — From the end of June to the middle of August.

LARVA. — On *Poa pratensis* and other grasses, in April and May.

VARIETY. — v. **Hispulla.**

Larger than the type; male darker; and has a more distinct patch of black scales beneath the median nervure of the f.-w.; h.-w. more dentate. The female has fulvous spread over a greater part of the f.-w.

HABITAT. — It is found in the same localities as the type, and is not uncommon. Specimens intermediate between type and variety often occur.

Hispulla is only found in Southern Europe.

E. Ida.

TIMES OF APPEARANCE. — June and July.

HABITAT. — Nice, in the Vallon des Fleurs, Vallon Obscur, and other spots; it is also to be met with in the mountainous parts of the district. On June 21st 1890,

I caught a ♂, very worn, in this spot; it had apparently been hybernating since the preceding season.

LARVA.— On *Triticum cæspitosa* and other grasses, in April and May.

E. Tithonus.

TIMES OF APPEARANCE. — July and August.

HABITAT. — Is found in the same localities as the last, which it otherwise greatly resembles in appearance and habits.

OVUM. — The eggs may be described as truncated cones; they stand erect, the base being broader than the apex; they have from sixteen to eighteen perpendicular ribs, and a great number of extremely delicate transverse striae; their colour at first is canary-yellow, but in a few days they acquire a browner hue, &c............— Condensed from *Newman*.

LARVA. — On *Poa annua* and other grasses, in May and June.

E. Pasiphœ.

TIMES OF APPEARANCE. — June and July.

HABITAT. — Millière says, "It is not rare in the glades of the small mountains."

LARVA. — On Grasses, in May.

E. Hyperanthus.

TIMES OF APPEARANCE. — June and July.

HABITAT.— Common in fresh and wooded situations. I have taken it in the fields below the Chemin de Venanson.

On July 11th 1890, I captured *Hyperanthus* in this latter spot, when they were abundant.
Ovum. — Is laid singly, in July and August.
Larva. — On *Poa annua* and other Grasses, but especially the former, in May and June.
Variety. — ab. **Arete**.
The black spots and yellow rings are entirely wanting on the u.-s., only the white spots being present. Occasionally even the white spots are absent.
Habitat. — Same localities as the type. Not very common.

Genus 7. — CŒNONYMPHA

C. Iphis.
Times of Appearance. — July and August.
Habitat. — At Saint-Martin-Vésubie : Mt. Balme de la Frema, not far from the summit.
On July 24th 1889, I captured several ♂ and ♀ in this spot, and in the following season I caught two ♂ and three ♀, also in the same locality.
Larva. — On Grasses, in April and May.
Observation. — Local ; but common where it occurs. Many of the ♂ have the ocellated spots on the u.-s. of the h.-w. in abeyance, and sometimes occasionally altogether absent. Perhaps a distinct variety.

C. Arcania.
Times of Appearance. — June and July.
Habitat. — At Saint-Martin-Vésubie: on Mts. Palù, Colmiane and Conchet, Route de Venanson, frequenting in preference the shade of the hazel bushes.

Larva. — On different Grasses, especially *Melica ciliata*, in May.

Pupa. — "In the middle of May, the caterpillar changes to a reddish brown pupa, without angles or tubercles, and rather rounded in shape. It is suspended."— *Lg*.

Variety. — v. **Darwiniana**.
Rather smaller than the type, the white band on the u.-s. of the h.-w. narrower, and of the same width throughout.

Observation. — Common ; but local.

C. Dorus.

Time of Appearance. — July.

Habitat. — Nice, &c., in the Vallon Obscur ; and at Saint-Martin-Vésubie, where it is common, especially on the Chemin de Venanson, and the Route de Saint-Martin, on the ascent to the Balme.

I have frequently seen little groups of eight or ten, hovering over some plant or other attractive object.

Larva. — On *Agrostis*, in June.

Observation. — I possess a ♂ of *Dorus*, which was taken in the mountains, some years ago, in which the black spot near the apex is considerably enlarged, about twice the normal size.

This dot is surrounded with a *distinct* light fulvous ring. Most of the specimens I have hitherto met with have this ring hazy. The number of spots also are often inconstant.

C. Pamphilus.

Times of Appearance. — May to September.

Habitat. — Common everywhere.

Ovum. — Round, and green.

Larva. — On Grasses, especially *Cynosurus cristatus*, from April to September.

On May 7th 1891, I obtained a caterpillar of this species from the ovum.

The larva changed to a pupa on July 18th, fastened to a blade of grass in the interior of the breeding-cage.

An imago (of the *var. Lyllus*) emerged on August 2nd. The stages, from the birth of the caterpillar to the exit of the perfect insect from the chrysalis, had thus occupied exactly twelve weeks and four days.

It moulted its skin four times. The following will give an idea of the intervals occupied in this process.

1st moult............................	May 19th.
2nd do.	June 7th.
3rd do.	July 6th.
4th when it finally discarded its skin, to assume the chrysalis state.........	" 18th.

Pupa. — " Sometimes uniform green, sometimes with three black lines on the wing cases, anal point reddish ; round, and without angular projections."— *Lg. But. Eur.*, vol. I, p. 310.

Mine had the numerous black markings (I counted fifteen), among them a faint dorsal line. In length, it was 4 1/2′′′, and in girth it measured 2′′′.

Variety. — v. **Lyllus**.

Larger and brighter than the type, and the apical spot is very distinct.

Habitat. — Same localities as the type.

It is common, sometimes almost replacing the type.

Family 10. — HESPERIDÆ

Genus 1. — SPILOTHYRUS

S. Alceæ.

TIMES OF APPEARANCE. — May, July and August.

HABITAT. — It is abundant, both on the coast and at Saint-Martin.

LARVA. — Feeds spun up in the leaves of different species of *Malvaceae*, in May and September.

According to Girard, those individuals appearing in the autumn hybernate in the hollow stems of Thistles and Burdocks.

VARIETY. — v. **Australis.**

Smaller than the type, and suffused to a greater extent with reddish brown.

S. Altheæ.

TIMES OF APPEARANCE. — May and August.

HABITAT. — Vallon Obscur, at Nice.

On May 5th 1891, I captured a specimen of the type *Altheae*, in this locality. It has been sent to Staudinger, and is undoubtedly correctly so designated, although the European works state that it is only found " in Central and South-Eastern Europe."

LARVA. — (of the type). Unknown.

VARIETY. — v. **Baeticus.**

Smaller than *Altheae* and lighter, being of a yellowish or brownish colour.

HABITAT. — In the books, it is said to occur in " South-Western Europe." I suppose it is found on the Riviera, in the same localities as the typical form.

LARVA. — On *Marrubium Hispanicum*.
OBSERVATION. — This plant is not native to the department; though the genus *Marrubium* is represented. *(See Appendix).*

S. Lavateræ.

TIMES OF APPEARANCE. — May, and from July to the end of August.

HABITAT. — Vallon Obscur, Nice, &c.; and in the mountains at Saint-Martin-Vésubie, where, however, it is perhaps less common than at the coast. Fairly abundant.

OVUM. — Oval throughout its entire length, and delicately striated transversely ; faint yellow, with a slight iridescent glint. It is laid lengthways and singly on the hairy calyx of a bud, generally near the top of the flower-head, and is imperceptible unless on a near examination, between the closely placed buds.

I have found eggs in the early part of the month of July.

LARVA. — On *Stachys recta*, in May.

OBSERVATION. — The species is found on dry, calcareous and rocky ground. Millière notices this butterfly's habit of frequenting the edges of puddles.

Genus 2. — SYRICHTHUS

S. Proto ?

TIMES OF APPEARANCE. — June and July.

HABITAT. — Should be found in the same localities as the preceding. I have never yet taken it.

LARVA. — On *Phlomis lychnitis*, in April and May.

S. Tessellum.

TIMES OF APPEARANCE. — May and August.
HABITAT. — Millière states it to be " Rare."

S. Sidæ.

TIMES OF APPEARANCE. — May and June.
HABITAT. — It frequents woods and is somewhat uncommon, though not so rare as the last.
Millière enumerates the species in his *Catalogue*.
LARVA. — Unknown.

S. Carthami.

TIMES OF APPEARANCE. — May and August.
HABITAT. — Saint-Martin-Vésubie, Cascade and Madone. It is an alpine species, and does not occur on the coast. Common.
LARVA. — Unknown.

S. Alveus.

TIMES OF APPEARANCE. — May and August.
HABITAT. — Fairly common everywhere.
It is to be found in the mountains, as well as by the coast.
LARVA. — Unknown.
VARIETIES. — v. **Cirsii**,
v. **Carlinae**
and v. **Onopordii**.

The two latter of these is mentioned by Millière.

Cirsii is smaller than the type, the white spots on f.-w. rather more distinct ; h.-w. with a central and submarginal white band. U.-S.: h.-w. have the white bands narrower than in the type, the ground colour being of a darker green.

Habitat. — Same as the type.

v. Carlinae is smaller than *Aloeus* and darker, the spots on f.-w., indistinct and small. U.-S.: f.-w. grey, with small black and white spots ; h.-w. greenish with white spots, as in the typical form of the species.

Habitat. — "Cascade of the Borréon ; steep banks of the high Spaillard. Rather rare."— *Mil.*

v. Onopordii : Larger and darker than the typical insect, with white and black spots.

Habitat. — Same as *Aloeus*.

S. Serratulæ ?

Times of Appearance. — June and July.

Habitat. — Ought to occur in the Maritime Alps ; it is a meridional species.

Larva. — Unknown.

S. Cacaliæ.

Time of Appearance. — July.

Habitat.—" Spurs and summit of the Pic-de-l'Aigle, where it is very abundant on the flowering lavenders." — *Mil.*

Larva. — Unknown.

Observation.— It is an alpine species, and is found, according to Dr Hofmann, at altitudes varying from 1.900 mètres (3280 feet), to 2,300 m. (7544 ft.)

S. Malvæ.

Aloeolus ; Hub., Godt.

Times of Appearance. — May and August.

Habitat. — Generally distributed.

Ovum. — The eggs are small, round, and of a pale green colour. Each egg is deposited singly on the upper surface of the leaves, or on the stems of the plant.

Larva. — On *Rubus fruticosus, R. idaeus* (Raspberry), *Fragaria vesca*, and according to Dr Ernst Hofmann, of Stuttgart, on *Potentilla comarum*, in April and September.

Variety. — ab. **Taras.**
This form is distinguished, among other things, by the white spots on the f.-w., which are very large and confluent, giving the wing the appearance of being white in the central portion, with black veins.

S. Sao.
Times of Appearance. — May, July and August.
Habitat. — Nice, Cannes and other places on the coast line ; also in the mountains. It appears commonest in the southern area of its distribution, and is rather scarcer in the mountainous parts.
Larva. — Unknown.

Genus 3. — NISONIADES

N. Tages.
Times of Appearance. — April and August.
Habitat. — Commonly distributed.
Ovum. — Eggs in May.
Larva. — On *Lotus corniculatus* and *Eryngium campestre*, in May, June and September.

Genus 4. — HESPERIA

H. Thaumas.
   Linea, Hub. Godt.
Times of Appearance. — June to September.
Habitat. — Common.

Ovum. — In July; the young larvae which come forth probably hybernating.

Larva. — On grasses, especially *Piptaterum multiflorum*, in May and June.

Observation. — *Thaumas* is, perhaps, the most abundant of all the *Hesperidae*.

H. Lineola.

Times of Appearance. — July and August.

Habitat. — It is found in the same places as *Thaumas*, but is not so common.

Larva. — On grasses, in May and June.

H. Acteon.

Times of Appearance. — June to August.

Habitat. — Fairly abundant everywhere.

I have seen it in quantities, generally near water, in the Vallon Obscur, at the end of June (from 22nd onwards). It congregates in little groups on the moisture.

Larva. — On *Calamagrostis epigeios* and other Grasses, in June. It feeds at night.

Observation. — The ♀ is much less common than the ♂. It is distinguished, among other traits, by the absence of the small blackish streak in the centre of the f.-w.

H. Sylvanus.

Timés of Appearance. — May, June and August.

Habitat. — Generally distributed.

It seems partial to dry woods.

LARVA. — On *Holcus lanatus* and other Grasses, in May.

H. Comma.
TIMES OF APPEARANCE. — July and August.

HABITAT. — Common everywhere, both in the mountains and on the coast.

LARVA. — On *Lotus, Coronilla, Ornithopus* and other *Leguminosae*, in June and July.

H. Nostrodamus ?
TIMES OF APPEARANCE. — August.

HABITAT. — It should occur in the district, as it is stated in the larger works, as inhabiting among other places " the South of Europe generally." I have never found it ; and rather doubt its existence here, though perhaps it may fly in some unexplored corner of the department. It is essentially a southern species, and does not occur north of the Alps.

LARVA. — Unknown.

Genus 5. — CYCLOPIDES
Steropes. Boisd.

C. Morpheus.
Steropes ; Esp, Hüb.
Aracinthus ; Fab, Godt.

TIMES OF APPEARANCE. — The end of June and beginning of July.

HABITAT. — " Heights of Berthemont-les-Bains ; not very common."— *Mil.*

LARVA. — On Grasses, in May and June.

Genus 6. — CARTEROCEPHALUS

Cyclopides, Steropes, auctorum.

C. Palæmon.
Paniscus ; Fab, Esp, Godt.
TIMES OF APPEARANCE. — May and June.
HABITAT. — According to P. Millière, it is found in the " Valley of Lantosque. In grassy places, where it is not rare."
LARVA.—On *Plantago major,* in April and September.

BIBLIOGRAPHICAL LIST

As .... Asmus.
Bell .... Bell.
Boisd .... Boisduval.
Bork .... Borkhansen.
Dal .... Dalman. 1816 and 1823.
Dun .... Duncan, James, Foreign Butterflies.
　　　　　　 Entomologist, The, edited by Richard South
　　　　　　 F. E. S., no. 344., 1892.
Ev .... Eversmann. Bulletin de la Société Impériale des Naturalistes de Moscou.
Fab .... Fabricius. Entomologica Systematica Emendata et Aucta, Paris, 1793.
Godt .... Godt. Histoire Naturelle des Lépidoptères de France, Tome I. — V.
Hof .... Hofmann, Dʳ Ernst, Die Gross-Schmetterlinge Europas. Stuttgart, 1887. Coloured Plates.
H.-S .... Herrich-Schäffer.
Kir .... Kirby, W. F. A Manual of European Butterflies. London, 1862.
Lg. .... Lang, Henry C., M. D., F. L. S., &c. The Butterflies of Europe.Two volumes, 80 coloured plates. London, 1884.
Linn .... Linnaeus.
Mil .... Millière, Pierre, Iconographie et description des Chenilles et Lépidoptères inédits.
Mil .... Millière, P. Catalogue Raisonné des Lépidoptères du département des Alpes-Maritimes. (From the *Mémoires de la Société des Sciences Naturelles de Cannes*.Three parts. Pt. I only, deals with the Rhopalocera, as does also a portion of the Appendix. Cannes; (No date).

Newman ..... Newman, Edward F. L. S., F. Z. S., An Illustrated Natural History of British Butterflies, London ; (No date).
Oberth .... Oberthür.
Och .... Ochsenheimer. Die Schmetterlinge von, Europa. Leipzig, (1). — Ten volumes.
Och .... Ochsenheimer, 1807, (2) 1808., I to IV., Leipzig, 1807-1816.
Ram .... Rambur., Catalogue Systématique des Lépidoptères de l'Andalousie : Paris, Part. I, 1858.
Ram .... Rambur., Faune Entomologique de l'Andalousie : Paris 1838-39.
Risso .... Risso, A. Histoire Naturelle des principales productions des environs de Nice.
Stain .... Stainton, H. T., A Manual of British Butterflies and Moths.(Illustrations). London, 1857-1859. A portion of vol. I only, treats of the diurnal lepidoptera.
Stgr. or Staud. Staudinger, Otto, Ph. D. Catalogue ou énumération méthodique des Lépidoptères qui habitent le Territoire de la Faune Européenne. I., Macro-lepidoptera. Dresde, 1871. (This, together with Dr Wocke's Catalogue of the Micro-lepidoptera, which forms Part II of the same volume, is undoubtedly the most complete and accurate guide to the Lepidoptera of the European Fauna that has ever been written.)
V. G .... De Villiers and Guenée, Tableaux Synoptiques des Lépidoptères d'Europe, Tome I., Diurni, 1835.
Z .... Zeller.

INDEX OF FAMILIES

All synonymic names are italicised.

	PAGE		PAGE
Anthocaris	13	Nemeobius	48
Apatura	51	Nisoniades	98
Aporia	10	Œneis	80
Argynnis	62	Papilio	5
Cœnonympha	91	Pararge	86
Carterocephalus	101	Parnassius	8
Charaxes	50	Pieris	10
Colias	19	Polyommatus	29
Cyclopides	100	Rhodocera	21
Epinephile	88	Satyrus	81
Erebia	71	Spilothyrus	94
Hesperia	98	*Steropes*	
Leucophasia	18	Syrichthus	95
Libythea	49	Thais	7
Limenitis	53	Thecla	23
Lycaena	32	Thestor	29
Melanargia	69	Vanessa	53
Melitaea	57	*Zephyrus*	

INDEX OF SPECIES

VARIETIES AND SYNONYMS

The genus occurs after each species.
Species mentioned in the present work, but not belonging to the district, have an asterisk (*).
The synonyms of other writers, are in italics.

	PAGE
Acaciae, Thec	26
Actaea, Sat	85
Acteon, Hesp	99
Adippe, Arg	66
Adrasta, Par	87
Aegeria, Par	88
Aegon, Lyc	33
Aëllo, Oen	80
Aesculi, Thec	26
Aethiops, Ereb	78
Aglaja, Arg	65
Alceae, Spil	94
Alcon, Lyc	44
Alcyone, Sat	81
Alexanor, Pap	5
Allionia, Sat	84
Allous, Lyc	36
Altheae, Spil	94
Alveolus, Syr	97
Alveus, Syr	96
Amanda, Lyc	38
Anargyra, Arg	67
Antiopa, Van	56
Apollo, Parn	8
Aracinthus, Cycl	100
Arcania, Coen	91
Arcas, Lyc	47
Arete, Epin	91
Argiolus, Lyc	41
Argus, Lyc	34

	PAGE
Argyrognomon, Lyc	34
Arion, Lyc	45
Astrarche, Lyc	36
Atalanta, Van	56
Athalia, Melit	61
Aurinia, Melit	58
Ausonia, Anth	14
Australis, Spil	94
Ballus, Thestor	29
Baton, Lyc	34
Belia, Anth	13
Bellargus, Lyc	39
Bellidice, Pier	13
Bellezina, Anth	15
Betulae, Thec	23
Baeticus, Spil	94
Boetica, Lyc	32
Brassicae, Pier	10
Briseis, Sat	82
Bryoniae, Pier	12
Bubastis, Ereb	72
Cacaliae, Syr	97
Caecodromus, Ereb	75
C-album, Van	54
Callidice, Pier	12
Camilla, Lim	53
Cardamines, Anth	15
Cardui, Van	57
Carlinae, Syr	96
Carthami, Syr	96

INDEX OF SPECIES

Name	PAGE
Cassandra, Thais	7
Cassiope, Ereb	71
Celtis, Lib	49
Ceronus, Lyc	39
Cerri, Thec	26
Ceto, Ereb	73
Charlotta, Arg	65
Cinnus, Lyc	39
Cinxia, Melit	59
Circe, Sat	81
Cirsii, Syr	96
Cleodoxa, Arg	67
Cleopatra, Rhod	21
Clytie, Apat	51
Cœlestina, Lyc	43
Confluens, Pol	30
Cordula, Sat	86
Corydon, Lyc	39
Corythalia, Melit	61
Crataegi, Apor	10
Cyanecula, Lyc	45
Cyllarus, Lyc	43
Cynthia, Melit	57
Damon, Lyc	41
Daphne, Arg	64
Daplidice, Pier	13
Darwiniana, Cœnon	92
Dejone, Arg	60
Desfontaines, Melit	58
* Desfontanii, Melit	59
Dia, Arg	63
Didyma, Melit	60
Diniensis, Leuc	18
Dolus, Lyc	40
Donzelii, Lyc	41
Dorilis, Pol	30
Dorus, Cœnon	92
Dromus, Ereb	75
Dryas, Sat	84
Duponchelii, Leuc	18
Edusa, Col	20
Egea, Van	53
Egerides, Par	88
Eleus, Pol	31
* Epiphron, Ereb	71
Epistygne, Ereb	74
Eris, Arg	66
Erynis, Ereb	76
Erysimi, Leuc	18
Escheri, Lyc	38
Eumedon, Lyc	38
Eupheno, Anth	18
Euphenoides, Anth	16
Euphrosyne, Arg	62
Europomene, Col	19
Euryale, Ereb	80
Eurybia, Pol	30
Evias, Ereb	74
Farinosa, Rhod	21
Fidia, Sat	84
* Galathea, Melan	69
Galene, Melan	69
Goante, Ereb	76
Gordius, Pol	30
Gorge, Ereb	75
Gorgone (Boisd), Ereb.	76
Gorgone (H.-S.), Ereb.	76
Gorgophone	72
Hecate, Arg	64
Helice, Col	20
Hermione, Sat	81
Hippothoë, Pol	30
Hispulla, Epin	89
Hyale, Col	20
Hygiaea, Van	56
Hyperanthus, Epin	90
Iberica, Melit	58
Icarinus, Lyc	37
Icarus, Lyc	36
* Ichnusa, Van	55
Ida, Epin	89
* Ilia, Apat	51
* Ilicis, Thec	26
Io, Van	56
Iolas, Lyc	44
Iphis, Cœnon	91
Iris, Apat	51
J.-Album	53
Janira, Epin	89
Jasius, Char	50
Joides, Van	56
Jole, Apat	51

VARIETIES AND SYNONYMS

	PAGE		PAGE
Lathonia, Arg	65	Pamphilus, Cœnon	92
Lathyri, Leuc	18	Pandora, Arg	68
Lavaterae, Spil	95	*Paniscus*, Cart	101
* Ledereri, Thec	27	Panoptes, Lyc	34
Lefebvrei, Lyc	40	Paphia, Arg	67
Leucomelas, Melan	69	Parthenie, Melit	61
Ligea, Ereb	79	Pasiphae, Epin	90
Lineola, Hesp	99	Peas, Sat	86
Lorquinii, Lyc	42	Pelopia, Melit	66
Lucina, Nem	48	*Phaedra*, Sat	84
Lycaon, Epin	88	Phicomone, Col	19
Lyllus, Cœnon	93	Phlaeas, Pol	31
Lynceus, Thec	24	Phœbe, Melit	59
* Lyssa, Parar	88	Phorcys, Ereb	73
Machaon, Pap	6	Pirata, Sat	82
Maera, Parar	86	* Podarce, Sat	86
Malvae, Syr	97	Podalirius, Pap	5
Manto, Ereb	72	Polychloros, Van	54
Medesicaste, Thais	8	Polyxena, Thais	7
Medusa, Ereb	73	Procida, Melan	69
Megaera, Parar	87	Proto, Syr	95
Melampus, Ereb	71	Provincialis, Melit	58
Melanops, Lyc	44	Pruni, Thec	26
Meleager, Lyc	40	*Psyche*, Melan	70
Menaclas, Lyc	41	Pyrenaica, Ereb	74
* Meridionalis, Melit	60	Quercus, Thec	28
Metis, Apat	52	Rapae, Pier	11
Minima, Lyc	42	Rhamni, Rhod	21
Mithridates, Lyc	40	Ripartii, Lyc	40
Mnemosyne, Parn	9	Roboris, Thec	27
Mnestra, Ereb	72	Rubi, Thec	28
Morpheus, Cycl	100	* Rumina, Thais	8
Napaeae, Pier	12	Sao, Syr	98
Napaea, Arg	63	Schmidtii, Pol	31
Napi, Pier	11	Sebrus, Lyc	42
Neoridas, Ereb	77	Semele, Sat	83
Niobe, Arg	00	Semiargus, Lyc	43
Nostrodamus, Hesp	100	Sidae, Syr	96
Ochracea, Thais	7	Simplonia, Anth	14
Omphale, Pol	29	Sinapis, Leuc	18
Onopordii, Syr	96	Sphyrus, Pap	7
Orbitulus, Lyc	35	Spini, Thec	24
Orion, Lyc	34	Statilinus, Sat	83
Palaemon, Cart	101	*Steropes*, Cycl	100
Palaeno, Col	19	Stevenii, Lyc	40
Pales, Arg	62	Stygne, Ereb	73

	PAGE		PAGE
Subalpina, Pol	31	Tithonus, Epin	90
Syllius, Melan	70	Tyndarus, Ereb	74
Sylvanus, Hesp	99	Urticae, Van	55
Tages, Nison	98	Valdensis, Arg	65
* Tagis, Anth	15	Valezina, Arg	67
Taras, Syr	98	Varia, Melit	62
Telicanus, Lyc	32	Virgaureae, Pol	29
Tessellum, Syr	96	W-album, Lyc	25
Testudo, Van	54	Werdandi, Col	19
Thaumas, Hesp	98	Zancleus, Pap	5
* Thersamon, Pol	29		

APPENDIX

A List of Latin names of Plants, with their English synonyms.

Agrostis canina.................	Small Bent-grass.
Aira cœspitosa.................	(See Triticum cœspitosa).
,, *praecox*....................	Vernal Hair-grass.
Amygdalus......................	Almond.
Anethum fœniculum.............	Fennel.
Anthoxanthum...................	Sweet Anthoxanth.
Anthyllis vulneraria............	Kidney Vetch ; Lady's Fingers.
Arabis alpina...................} *ciliata*....................}	Fringed Rockcress.
Arbutus unedo..................	Strawberry Tree.
Aristolochia....................	Birthwort.
Armeria vulgaris...............	Common Thrift.
Artemesia.......................	Artemesia.
Astragalus......................	Milk Vetch ; Astragal.
Avena elatior...................} *Arrhenatherum aveneceum*......}	False Oat ; Silver Oat-grass.
Betula...........................	Birch.
Brachypodium pinnatum.........	Heath False-Brome.
Bromus..........................	Brome Grass.
Calamagrostis epigeios..........	Wood Smallreed.
Calluna.........................	Heath.
Capparis........................	Caper.
Cardamine pratense............	Meadow Bittercress; Ladies' Smock; Cuckooflower.
,, *impatiens*...........	Narrow-leaved Cardamine, or Bitter Cress.
Carduus.........................	Thistle.
Celtis australis.................	Nettle Tree.
Centranthus ruber..............	Red Valerian.
Centaurea jacea................} ,, *nigra*................}	Black Centaurea.
Cerasus.........................	Cherry.
Comarum palustre..............} *Potentilla comarum*.............}	Marsh Potentil.
Coronilla........................	Coronilla.
Corydalis.......................	Corydal.
Corylus.........................	Hazel.
Crataegus oxyacantha...........	Hawthorn ; May ; Whitethorn.
Cynosurus cristatus.............	Crested Dog's Tail.
Cytisus.........................	Broom.
Dactylis........................	Cock's Foot.
Digitalis purpurea..............	Purple Foxglove.
Daucus carota..................	Wild Carrot.
Echium vulgare.................	Viper's Bugloss.
Erodium cicutarium.............	Stork's-bill.
Eryngium campestre............	Field Eryngo.
Festuca ovina...................	Sheep's Fescue.
Fragaria vesca..................	Strawberry.

Genista............................	Genista.
Geranium pratense...............	Blue Meadow Crane's-bill.
,, purpureum............	Crimson Crane's-bill.
,, sanguineum...........	
Hedera............................	Ivy.
Hieracium Pilosella..............	Mouse-ear Hawkweed.
Hippocrepis	Horseshoe Vetch.
Holcus lanatus...................	Meadow Soft-grass.
Humulus lupulus.................	Hop.
Iberis.............................	Candytuft.
Ilex...............................	Holly.
Inula.............................	Elecampane.
Lathyrus	Pea.
Linaria...........................	Toad-flax.
Ligustrum........................	Privet.
Lolium perenne	Rye-grass ; Common Ray-grass.
Lonicera..........................	Honeysuckle.
Lotus corniculatus................	Bird's foot trefoil.
Lythrum salicaria................	Purple Loosestrife.
Marrubium.......................	Horehound.
Medicago lupulina................	Black Medick.
Melampyrum.....................	Cow-wheat.
,, sylvaticum..........	Common Melampyre.
,, pratense............	
Melica............................	Melick.
Melilotus officinalis	Common Melilot.
Milium............................	Millet Grass.
Gastridum lendig rum...........	
Onobrychis sativa................	Sainfoin ; Saint-foin.
Hedysarum onobrychis...........	
Ononis spinosa...................	Restharrow.
Origanum vulgare...............	Wild Marjoram.
Ornithopus.......................	Bird's-foot.
Panicum sanguinale..............	Fingered Panic.
Parietaria officinalis.............	Wall Pellitory.
Phleum pratense.................	Timothy Grass ; Cat's Tail.
Piptaterum multiflorum..........	
Milium multiflorum..............	Millet Grass.
Agrostis miliacea.................	
Pisum sativum...................	Common Garden Pea.
Plantago	Plantain, and Scabious.
,, major...................	Greater Plantain.
,, lanceolata..............	Ribwort Plantain.
Poa annua........................	Annual Meadow Grass.
,, pratensis	Smooth-stalked Meadow Grass.
Polygonum bistorta...............	Bistort ; Snakeweed.
Populus alba.....................	White Poplar.
,, tremula	Aspen Poplar.
Primula veris....................	Common Primrose.
,, elatior...................	Oxlip.
Prunus communis................	Sloe ; Blackthorn.
Pyrus communis..................	Pear.
,, malus	Crab, and Apple Trees.
,, aria	White Beam.
,, Sorbus Aria..............	
Quercus ilex......................	Evergreen Oak.
,, robur....................	British Oak.
Resedaceae.......................	Mignonnette, etc.
Reseda luteola....................	Weld ; Dyer's Weed ; Dyer's Rocket ; Dyer's Mignonnette.
Rhamnus frangula................	Alder Buckthorn.
,, catharticus..............	Common Buckthorn.
Ribes rubrum.....................	Red and White Currant.
Rosa	Rose.

Robinia Pseudo-Acacia........	Acacia ; Robinia.
Rubus idaeus..................	Raspberry.
Rubus fruticosus..............	Bramble Blackberry ; Blackberry
Rumex acetosa................ " *acetosella*............	} Sheep-sorrel Dock.
" *hydrolapathum*........	Water Dock.
Salix alba....................	Common Willow ; Sallow.
Sanguisorba officinalis.........	Great Burnet.
Saxifraga.....................	Saxifrage.
Scabiosa succisa	Devil's bit.
Sedum telephium...............	Orpine Sedum.
Sisymbrium....................	Hedge-mustard.
Solidago virgaurea.............	Golden-rod.
Stachys.......................	Wound-wort.
Teucrium Scorodonia...........	Wood Sage.
Thymus vulgaris............... " *serpyllum*............	} Wild Thyme.
Trifolium......................	Clover ; Trefoil.
Triticum cœspitosum........... *Aria cœspitosua*.............. *Deschampsia*	} Tufty Hair Grass.
Triticum repens................	Couchgrass.
Tropaeolum....................	Nasturtium.
Turritis glabra................ *Arabis perfoliata*..............	} Tower-mustard; Tower-cress; Tower-wort. Glabrous Rockcress.
Ulex..........................	Furze.
Ulmus campestris...............	Elm ; Common Elm.
" *montana*	Wych Elm.
Urtica dioica...................	Common Nettle.
Vaccinium uliginosum...........	Bog Vaccinium.
Veronica......................	Veronica.
Vicia cracca...................	Tufted Vetch.
Viola odorata..................	Sweet Violet.
" *canina*..................	Dog Violet.
" *tricolor*	Heartsease ; Pansy.

ADDITIONS AND CORRECTIONS

Page **8**, after line 6 from top of page, insert " It is found even as high as Duranus, where I met with a ♀, slightly worn, by the road-side. Larvae also, were met with at this date (June 3rd 1892), some of them being nearly half-grown."

P. **22**, line 2 from top, read " and occurs even above Venanson."

P. **27**, after line 18 from top of page, insert " In some years it is even abundant. In the present season (1892), no less than twenty-nine specimens were taken ! It is noteworthy that there were none of the trees on which the species subsists in the larval state in the vicinity, though hazel *(Corylus)* and privet *(Ligustrum)* abounded.

" Possibly *Roboris* may feed, in addition to its known food-plants, on one or both of these ? "

P. **30**, line 15 from the top, reads **P. Alciphron v. Gordius**.

P. **30**, after line 21 from top, insert :

" VARIETY. — There is a form having fewer spots than the type, thus corresponding to the *var. Neera* of *Melitaea Didyma*. The u.-s. of the h.-w., especially, have only the double hind-marginal row of dots, all spots intervening, with the exception of the central group being absent. "

P. **40**, line 9 from bottom of page, to read :
" At La Bollène. Several specimens, rather worn, were captured by my cousin, Edward C. Casey, in the above locality, on the hill-side near the main road, July 24th 1892. "

P. **61**, line 2 from top, insert " On *Linaria*."

P. **74**, after line 20 from top, read :

" E. Lappona, Esp.

" TIMES OF APPEARANCE. — July and August.

" HABITAT. — Summit of the Pepiori, near Saint-Martin-Vésubie, at a height of 2,675 mètres (8774 feet).

" It ascends to a greater elevation than any of the before-mentioned *Erebiae*, being only found on the verge of perpetual snow.

" I captured three specimens (two males and a female), rather worn, July 18th 1892, in the above-mentioned locality, and have never heard of any previous captures in the neighbourhood.

" VARIETIES. — ab. **Pollux**
and v. **Sthennyo**.

" In the former variety the wings are not banded beneath. *Sthennyo* hardly differs from the type.

" LARVA. — Unknown. "

P. **83**, after line 4 from top, read :

" S. Arethusa.

" TIMES OF APPEARANCE. — June and July.

" HABITAT. — Appears in dry and stony places, but is local. " — *Mil*.

" I met with a fresh ♂ specimen apparently intermediate between the type and the *var. Dentata*, on the Route de Venanson, Saint-Martin-Vésubie, August 7th 1892.

"Variety. — v. **Dentata**, Stgr.

"U.-s. : h.-w. with neuration marked with white; also a clear white central band, and usually a darkish dentate line between it and the hind-margin.

"Habitat. — In these alps it is found in the same places as the typical insect.

"Larva. — Unknown."

www.ingramcontent.com/pod-product-compliance
Lightning Source LLC
Chambersburg PA
CBHW020131170426
43199CB00010B/716